balances work and life

For more than 20 years, millions of businessmen and women have followed the advice set out in Ken Blanchard's phenomenally popular One Minute Manager series. As this book shows, however, achieving balance in our lives is a crucial ingredient in ultimate success.

This is the story of a One Minute Manager who was so successful in every way that he forgot one important thing: to stay physically fit. He was so much in demand that he ate on the run, didn't take time to exercise, and all the while saw his weight balloon and his breath grow shorter. He soon discovered success in business was endangering his health - his life was out of balance. For all those busy, achieving people with overcrowded schedules, this useful blueprint shows how to manage stress and make a lifetime commitment to fitness and well-being.

Ken Blanchard is the founder and Chairman of The Ken Blanchard Companies. His One Minute Manager series has sold over 13 million copies and been translated into more than 25 languages. He has also written or co-authored numerous other books, including Gung Ho!, Big Bucks!, Raving Fans! and The One Minute Golfer.

D.W. Edington is a professor of kinesiology and Director of the Management Research Center at the University of Michigan. He has authored numerous articles and books, and his work in the field of health risk appraisal is considered to be the model for corporate development plans in the wellness area.

Marjorie Blanchard is co-founder of Blanchard Training and Development, Inc., and is a widely known and respected consultant, lecturer and trainer. She specializes in communication, leadership, health promotion, life planning and team building, and has been recognized as an American Express Speaker of the Year.

Other titles in this series:

THE ONE MINUTE MANAGER
Ken Blanchard and Spencer Johnson

PUTTING THE ONE MINUTE MANAGER TO WORK
Ken Blanchard and Robert Lorber

THE ONE MINUTE SALES PERSON
Spencer Johnson

LEADERSHIP AND THE ONE MINUTE MANAGER
Ken Blanchard, Patricia Zigarmi and Drea Zigarmi

THE ONE MINUTE MANAGER MEETS THE MONKEY
Ken Blanchard, William Oncken Jr. and Hal Burrows

THE ONE MINUTE MANAGER BUILDS HIGH PERFORMING TEAMS
Ken Blanchard, Donald Carew and Eunice Parisi-Carew

RAVING FANS!
Ken Blanchard and Sheldon Bowles

GUNG HO!
Ken Blanchard and Sheldon Bowles

BIG BUCKS!
Ken Blanchard and Sheldon Bowles

HIGH FIVE!
Ken Blanchard, Sheldon Bowles, Don Carew and Eunice Parisi-Carew

LEADERSHIP BY THE BOOK
Ken Blanchard, Bill Hybels and Phil Hodges

THE LITTLE BOOK OF COACHING
Ken Blanchard and Don Shula

THE ONE MINUTE APOLOGY
Ken Blanchard and Margret McBride

THE ON-TIME, ON-TARGET MANAGER
Ken Blanchard and Steve Gottry

THE ONE MINUTE GOLFER
Ken Blanchard

THE ONE MINUTE FATHER
Spencer Johnson

THE ONE MINUTE MOTHER
Spencer Johnson

the :01 One minute manager balances work and life

Invaluable advice for getting the most out of life

KEN BLANCHARD
D.W. EDINGTON
MARJORIE BLANCHARD
illustrations by RON WEIL
with FRANK EISENZIMMER

HarperCollins *Publishers*

HarperCollins*Publishers*
77–85 Fulham Palace Road,
Hammersmith, London W6 8JB
Published in the UK by
HarperCollins *Publishers* 2004

First published in the USA as
The One Minute Manager ® Gets *Fit* ™

Fifth impression 2010

ISBN 13: 978-0-00-735914-1

HarperCollins *Publishers*
A-53, Sector 57, NOIDA, Uttar Pradesh – 201301, India
77-85 Fulham Palace Road, London W6 8JB, United Kingdom
Hazelton Lanes, 55 Avenue Road, Suite 2900, Toronto, Ontario M5R 3L2
and 1995 Markham Road, Scarborough, Ontario M1B 5M8, Canada
25 Ryde Road, Pymble, Sydney, NSW 2073, Australia
31 View Road, Glenfield, Auckland 10, New Zealand
10 East 53rd Street, New York NY 10022, USA

Printed and bound at
Thomson Press (India) Ltd.

the One minute manager balances work and life

The Symbol

The One Minute Manager's symbol—a one-minute readout from the face of a modern digital watch—is intended to remind each of us to take a minute out of our day to look into the faces of the people we manage. And to realize that they are our most important resource.

Introduction

I am excited about republishing *The One Minute Manager® Gets Fit™* as part of the personal development series for The One Minute Manager® Library. I think renaming it *The One Minute Manager® Balances Work and Life* is appropriate as we move into the rapidly changing stress-inducing twenty-first century. Everyone is asking for help in a time when the only predictable things in life are death, taxes, and change.

In this episode of the One Minute Manager®, our hero has a different kind of visitor. He gets a call from a college professor who comes not to learn but to teach. In the process, the One Minute Manager learns that the key to getting balance in your life and managing stress is taking the time to work on your fitness and health. Not only does he learn that working on his physical well-being makes a real difference in his own life, but he realizes that through a health-promotion program he can make a significant impact on the satisfaction and performance of the people in his company. It becomes crystal clear to the One Minute Manager that healthy people not only feel good about themselves but they produce good results.

In many ways this book is my ongoing story. Ever since the phenomenal success of *The One Minute Manager®*, which I coauthored with Spencer Johnson, I have been dying from good opportunities. I had ballooned to 236 pounds, which, with my 5'11" frame, left me with only one thing to say: "I'm too short for my weight." That, combined with the fact I couldn't run down the block without panting for breath, made me a prime candidate to get my life back in balance. When I was writing this book, I learned that maintaining a healthy lifestyle is easier said than done.

To work on the book and my own fitness, I asked two very important people in my life to join me. First, a longtime friend and colleague, D. W. Edington, a Ph.D. in physical education with specialized training in biochemistry, who for over a decade has been heading up the physical-education division and the Health Management Research Center at the University of Michigan, Ann Arbor, and second, my wife, Marjorie Blanchard, a Ph.D. in communication studies, who is a recognized expert in health promotion, life planning, stress management, and leadership and has been consulting for over twenty years in entrepreneurial and *Fortune* 500 companies.

Both Dee and Margie have believed for a long time that working on your tone—physical well-being—can significantly help moderate stress and ensure balance in your life. They convinced me and I twisted the One Minute Manager's arm. We hope that after reading *The One Minute Manager® Balances Work and Life,* you will be committed to take charge of your life through health and fitness and then share this book with others at work and at home so it can make a difference with them too.

—KEN BLANCHARD

Dedicated
to
Marilyn P. Edington
a health promotion consultant
to corporations
for
her loving support and
encouragement of Dee
and their son, David,
and for her longtime commitment and
friendship
to Ken and Margie

and

The staff and graduate students
at the
Health Management Research Center
University of Michigan

Foreword

I was excited to learn that Ken Blanchard had decided to expand the scope of the ONE MINUTE MANAGER LIBRARY into health and fitness. First of all, I felt that if he and his co-authors, D. W. Edington and Marjorie Blanchard, could capture for adults the essence of the Olympic spirit of a sound mind and body in simple, easy-to-understand ways, as Ken has done with management concepts, this book would be a tremendous help to the health and fitness field.

Second, if in the process he could get himself in good health and fitness shape, Ken could prove that if you are committed to your own self-wellness, there is no excuse, not even the craziness of your schedule, that can stop your progress. To me the book and Ken have done both these things.

And one last thing. From my perspective as a medical doctor and expert on cardiovascular fitness, *The One Minute Manager® Balances Work and Life* is based on sound medical advice. So read and enjoy this book, but more important, put its concepts to work. They will add a dimension to your life that will help you move toward peak performance.

—IRVING I. DARDIK, M.D.
Founding Chairman
U.S. Olympic Committee
Sports Medicine Council

The One Minute Manager®
Balances Work and Life

ONE day as the One Minute Manager stood looking out his office window down onto the traffic, he found himself focused on the mail truck and the two people gathering up the letters and packages to be delivered. He thought to himself, "That would be an ideal job to have. All you have to do is pick up the mail in the morning and then deliver it to its appropriate destination. At the end of the day, you return to the post office with outgoing mail and then you are free to go home without a care in the world, until the next morning."

Now the One Minute Manager knew that mail delivery was more complicated than that, but seeing the truck ignited his yearning for simplicity in his life. Everything seemed to be out of whack lately. He had done so well in turning his last operation from a dying enterprise into an exciting, profitable venture that he had been given a larger company to tackle. Always striving to be the best, the One Minute Manager had jumped into his new job with both feet. "And believe me," he thought to himself, "this operation needed help."

The last manager had a style of "ready, fire, blame." As a result, people felt demoralized. They were continually being yelled at for not doing what they didn't know they were supposed to do in the first place. The One Minute Manager knew that before you could catch people doing things right and praise them, they had to have clear goals. So he had started a companywide goal-setting program.

These initial demands of turning around a bad situation were time consuming enough. But add the outside demands on his time—to speak and give advice to others because of his popularity as a manager—and suddenly twenty-four hours was not a long enough day for the One Minute Manager.

While all these opportunities were exciting, lately the One Minute Manager found himself losing energy and feeling more tired than ever before. He had even become irritable at home. In fact, his wife had said to him yesterday:

If
you don't
watch out,
success
could kill
you!

As he thought about the possible truth in that statement, the One Minute Manager's attention was interrupted by his intercom.

"There's a professor from the university on the phone," said his secretary. "He says it's important that he talk to you."

"About what?"

"He wouldn't say," said his secretary, "but he said something about you 'needing him.'"

"Needing him?" echoed the One Minute Manager. Curious, he picked up the phone. "Can I help you?"

"You probably can," said the professor, "but I think I can help you even more."

"That might be true," said the One Minute Manager, a little taken aback, "but what I don't need right now is another good opportunity."

"I know that," said the professor. "That's why I called."

"Who are you?"

"I'm the director of the Health Management Research Center," said the professor. "I'd like to share some information that I think could be useful to you. Do you have any time this week?"

"I used to answer that kind of question by saying 'anytime this week,' but I can't say that anymore. In fact, my time this week is completely taken. Next week I'm scheduled to be out of town for three days. This just isn't a good time for me to take on any new ideas or projects."

"I'm sorry to hear that," said the professor, "but I also know that forcing someone to look at his or her lifestyle doesn't work either. Why don't I call you in a couple of weeks?"

"That's fine," said the One Minute Manager. "Perhaps things will be less hectic then."

For the next ten days, the One Minute Manager forgot all about the professor's call, until the next Saturday night.

THE One Minute Manager and his wife went to bed about midnight after playing bridge with some friends. About 3:30 he woke up with a real pain in his chest and a lot of gas. He got up, went to the bathroom, and walked around, but it didn't seem to help. "It's probably just something I ate," rationalized the One Minute Manager. It annoyed him, though, that one of the first things he thought about was the professor's call and Charlie's death. Charlie was one of their best friends, who had died suddenly last summer at age forty-two, shocking everyone. Just as he was trying to get all this out of his mind, Alice woke up.

"What's going on?" she said.

"Oh, nothing."

"Are you telling me you just like to walk around at three-thirty in the morning? I've lived with you too long to believe that. Come clean."

"I just have some indigestion."

"Where?"

"It hurts a little here," said the One Minute Manager, pointing toward the center of his chest.

"That's a funny place for indigestion. Just sit down on the bed a moment. I want to talk with you."

"I don't want a lecture right now on my health and lifestyle."

"I'm not going to do that," said Alice. "I just want you to do me a favor."

"What is it?" said the One Minute Manager as he sat down.

"Honey, I was reading the other day that it takes on the average six hours after the first symptom before most heart attack victims get some medical help. Unfortunately, about fifty percent have done irreparable damage by then if they are not already dead. What I'd like us to do is just ride over to the emergency room and let them check you out. If it's only indigestion we'll be home and back in bed in forty-five minutes."

"That's silly," said the One Minute Manager. "I'm not having a heart attack!"

"I know it's silly. That's why I said I wanted you to do *me* a favor. It's just for me, not you. OK?"

Not wanting his wife to know he was getting a little concerned too, the One Minute Manager said, "If you put it like that, OK, but I'm only doing it for you."

"I appreciate that," said Alice. "Consider that I owe you one."

"You know I have a memory like an elephant," smiled the One Minute Manager.

When they got over to the emergency room at the nearby hospital, it was very quiet so the One Minute Manager was ushered in without much delay.

While he was on the table waiting for the doctor, all kinds of things were going through the One Minute Manager's mind. Since the pain and gas had not subsided, he even said a prayer or two with the usual "I promise to be good" ending that he used as a kid.

When the doctor showed up, he asked the One Minute Manager all kinds of questions while he took his blood pressure and tapped all around. Then the doctor suggested they do an EKG just to be on the safe side. The One Minute Manager hated those because the nurses had to either shave the hair on his chest to attach the electrodes or pull his hair when they took them off.

When the doctor finished, he told the One Minute Manager everything was OK but it was probably a blessing he had this warning. Some people never get one.

The One Minute Manager was relieved. On the way home he said to his wife, "I got a call before my last trip from some professor at the university who heads up a fitness center."

"What did he want?"

"He said he had some information that might be useful to me. I think I'll call him this week."

"I'd be interested in knowing what he has to say," said Alice.

On Monday the One Minute Manager called the professor and made an appointment for Wednesday.

WHEN the professor arrived at the One Minute Manager's office on Wednesday morning, he found him sitting quietly at his desk. The One Minute Manager looked up and smiled at the professor.

"Good morning, Doc. Good to see you!"

"I appreciate your willingness to talk with me," said the professor.

"It's my pleasure," said the One Minute Manager. "Sorry I didn't have time to talk to you a couple of weeks ago. You said you had some thoughts to share with me. What do you have in mind?"

"Let me start by asking you a question."

"Fire away."

"Would you like to be a peak performer with a stress-free life?" asked the professor.

"Who wouldn't like that?" answered the One Minute Manager, thinking about his own situation. "But I think it is unrealistic."

"It's not only unrealistic, but if you had a stress-free life, you'd be dead."

"So the issue," smiled the One Minute Manager, "is managing stress, not being afraid of it."

"Right," said the professor. "Stress in and of itself is not good or bad. It all depends on how you handle it. How well do you deal with stress?"

"Generally, pretty well. In fact, without some stress like a deadline or gaining someone's approval, I don't perform as well."

"How are you managing your stress right now?"

"Not so well lately. I never realized that success could bring just as much stress as, if not more than, failure."

"Are you thinking maybe you could die from good opportunities?" asked the professor emphatically.

"Exactly! While I think One Minute Management is beginning to become alive in this company and starting to take a good turn, all my outside demands have been draining. I don't seem to have much time anymore for myself or my family."

"I heard that was your situation. As I told you, that's why I called," said the professor. "I thought I might be able to help."

"What did you have in mind?"

"I'm interested in the concept of wellness. For a long time people have been saying that there is a direct relationship between the amount of stress in your life and your performance."

"I would guess that you have proved that relationship in recent years."

"Yes, we have. One of the things we know is that up to a certain point, there is a positive relationship between the amount of stress and increasing productivity. At that point—and it varies for everyone—productivity no longer goes up with stress. In fact, eventually performance begins to decline if there is too much stress."

"When that happens, does 'burnout' occur?"

"Yes," said the professor. "Burnout is a term often associated with too much stress."

"Why do people reach burnout?" asked the One Minute Manager.

"BECAUSE," responded the professor, "after a certain point, when stress continues to go up, so does strain—which is an emotional and physical reaction to stress. This stress/strain relationship can occur either at work or at home and, if permitted to build up, will not only result in declines in performance, but can eventually have a negative impact on health too."

"Is there ever a time when there is too little stress?"

"Yes, when you are understimulated at work or at home. We call that 'rustout.'"

"So you are looking for the right amount of stress and least amount of strain to give you the maximum amount of productivity," said the One Minute Manager. "I once completed a questionnaire in an airline magazine where you could add up your stress points. Different events, like the death of a spouse or being fired, got different points."

"I bet all the events were not negative," said the professor.

"No they weren't. Some of them were very positive, like getting married or being promoted."

"How was your stress count?"

"At that time it was fairly low," smiled the One Minute Manager. "Success had not reared its challenging head yet. Today it would be a different story. With my new promotion came all kinds of new responsibilities, as well as a physical move to a different house and town. In addition, I've been asked to give a number of speeches—something I've never done before. And besides, people are calling at all hours of the day to seek my advice or get me to do one thing or another. What can I do during this crazy time in my life to avoid getting seriously ill?"

"Why do you ask that?"

"Because now that you've got me thinking about the relationship between stress and health, I remember hearing that if stress and strain become too great in your life—and I'm starting to feel that way about my life—you can become seriously ill."

"That certainly is true from my experience," said the professor. "Too much stress can lead to ulcers, a heart attack, and even cancer if you don't find ways to buffer or protect yourself from the usual direct stress/strain relationship."

"You have my attention now," said the One Minute Manager. "Tell me more about how I can protect myself."

"We have found that there are four moderators to the stress/strain relationship," said the professor as he handed the One Minute Manager a little poster to read.

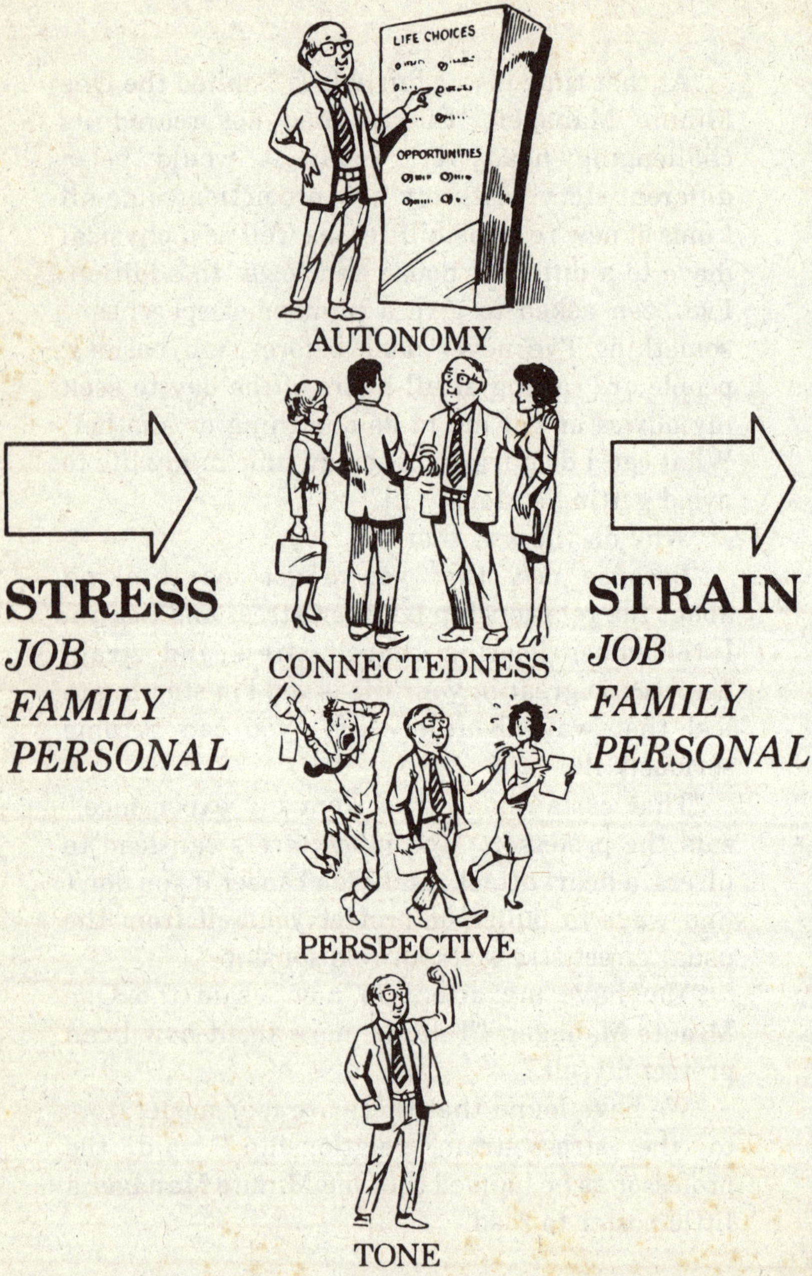
LIFE CHOICES
OPPORTUNITIES
AUTONOMY
CONNECTEDNESS
PERSPECTIVE
TONE
STRESS
JOB
FAMILY
PERSONAL
STRAIN
JOB
FAMILY
PERSONAL

WHEN the One Minute Manager finished looking at the card, the professor continued, "As I said, when stress increases at work or at home, so do strains. If both stress and strain continue to build up, illness can result. We have found that when the four moderators—autonomy, connectedness, perspective, and tone—are in good shape, they can help prevent stress from turning into strain. It is interesting that these moderators are the same ingredients people talk about when they are asked to describe peak periods in their lives—times when they were feeling exceptionally good, feeling on top of the world."

"Let's talk about these four moderators," said the One Minute Manager.

"The first one is autonomy," said the professor. "People who have a high sense of autonomy state that they have many choices and relatively good control in their lives. They see at least some of their daily activities as moving them toward their own important professional and personal goals."

"You mean their lives are not totally controlled by their job, a boss, a spouse, anyone or anything."

"You're right. Autonomy is the sense we often get on weekends when we have free time. Autonomy can also mean having the necessary skills and qualifications to be able to move from one job opportunity to another if we want to."

"I can see where having a high sense of autonomy would be a good stress moderator," said the One Minute Manager. "What's the next moderator?"

"Connectedness," said the professor. "People with a high sense of connectedness feel that they have strong, positive relationships at home, at work, and in the community and feel in tune with their surroundings as well."

"I certainly know how important it is to feel comfortable and welcome on the job," said the One Minute Manager. "Not to mention feeling part of the community and having a group of friends with whom you can let your hair down. Alice is feeling especially disconnected right now after our recent move to this new job and community. Just yesterday she told me she was out for a walk in the neighborhood and got tears in her eyes when she saw a woman walking down the street with a cup of coffee in her hand, obviously heading to a friend's house. Alice hasn't made any real friends yet."

"I remember those times, too," said the professor. "You get feelings like that when you go away for the weekend and you realize when you get home that no one knew you were gone, much less that you have come back."

"I know that when we make new friends, know our way around better, and have our house feeling like home again, we'll feel more connected," said the One Minute Manager. "What's the third moderator?"

"The third moderator is perspective. Perspective has to do with the meaning of life —the direction, the purpose, the passion that you feel for what you are doing."

"Does perspective keep you from letting little things get you down?"

"It sure does. Since you have a big picture of where you want your life to go, the normal stress and strains of daily life don't get blown up out of proportion. You can go into your 'zoo mentality' when necessary."

"Zoo mentality?" wondered the manager.

"I coined that term when my kids were young. They loved to go to the zoo, and I usually got the assignment because chasing kids around the park drives most parents crazy. I loved it because when I got into my zoo mentality, nothing the kids did would bother me. It always seemed strange to me that parents would take their kids to the zoo and spend the whole time yelling at them. Since I wanted to have fun with my kids and to have them see me as fun to be around, I was able to see beyond every little incident and enjoy the day because it was contributing to my goals."

"So perspective," said the One Minute Manager, "is having a good sense of where you're heading and seeing the total picture of your life so today takes on a special significance."

"That's right," said the professor, "and when perspective is high, you're on the way to a productive time in your life."

"What is the fourth moderator?"

"Tone," responded the professor. "How you feel about your body, your energy level, your physical well-being and appearance. In remembering or talking about exceptionally good periods in their lives, people invariably mention how they felt or looked physically—that they were ten pounds lighter or in great shape. We know that people can improve their tone through managing their lifestyles better—participating in exercise and weight-control programs. We also know that success in the tone area can definitely improve a person's overall self-esteem and, in the process, help moderate stress."

"I don't think you need to look at me very long," said the One Minute Manager, "to see how bad my tone is. I feel as if someone had blown me up like a balloon. And in terms of being in shape—forget it! I played golf the other day and almost died because they had run out of carts and we had to walk."

"I appreciate your honesty. I'm sure you would have a whole different attitude about the stress in your life if your tone were better."

"No doubt about it," said the One Minute Manager. "It seems to me that the four stress moderators you have been talking about could have a kind of a domino effect on each other."

"WHAT do you mean?" responded the professor.

"If you lose your balance and fall down on one, it can begin to knock the others down too."

"I hadn't thought of it as a domino effect," said the professor, "but that's what happens. If, for example, something changes on your job and you begin to lose your sense of autonomy, suddenly you start getting irritable with the people around you. You start complaining about your job, where you live, and all that."

"Then I imagine," said the One Minute Manager, "you may begin to lose perspective. You don't see as clearly where you are going."

"Exactly. And you start overeating and not exercising and pretty soon everything is out of whack."

"That's what has happened to me," said the One Minute Manager. "All my good opportunities, rather than increasing my autonomy, have made my life feel out of control, especially at home. The family has been getting the short end of the stick. You know how that goes. You keep thinking they'll understand."

"ISN'T that the truth," smiled the professor. "In the process of trying to respond to all the demands on my time, I think I have lost sight of where I am going—my perspective needs work. And as for tone, we've already covered that. I'm overweight and out of shape. I've been eating my way across the country and now have about fifty extra pounds. I'd be hard pressed to run a block without panting."

"Don't feel like the Lone Ranger. That's a common problem."

"If the domino effect is working and everything seems out of whack, as you say," wondered the One Minute Manager, "how do you turn it around?"

"We find the best place to start turning things around is with tone. You start to exercise and eat properly."

"Why do you start there?"

"Because the things that make up tone are often observable and measurable. You can count the miles you have run or walked, the pounds you have lost. As you contend, 'Feedback is the Breakfast of Champions,' and tone is the easiest moderator from which to generate specific feedback."

"That makes sense," said the One Minute Manager, "and if you can take the time to exercise and eat properly, you will begin to get back a sense of autonomy; after all, controlling your time has to do with autonomy."

"Right," said the professor. "And pretty soon you begin to regain a better sense of perspective. For some reason, while I am exercising I seem to be inspired to do some serious soul-searching and creative thinking about my life."

"That makes sense to me, but there is one moderator I can't see being improved by tone, and that is connectedness."

"That's an interesting one," said the professor. "Did you ever read the book *Positive Addiction* by William Glasser?"

"No," answered the One Minute Manager.

"Glasser studied joggers and meditators and the impact on their lives of the time they took each day for their activity. He found that these people, and others who took time for themselves every day to do something alone that was intrinsically good and noncompetitive, were able to be more empathetic and better able to listen to the concerns of others. Because they had taken care of themselves and were feeling good about themselves, it seems they could now more easily be with other people."

"That's fascinating," said the One Minute Manager. "So working on good tone *can* have an impact on connectedness, too. How do I get started? You've convinced me that better tone could help me shape up my whole life."

"THAT's what I hoped you would say," said the professor. "Why don't you come over to our Health Management Research Center at the university tomorrow afternoon and we can help you get started. Besides, I'd love to show you our facilities and have you meet some of our staff."

"That's a deal," said the One Minute Manager as he stood up and shook the professor's hand. "You've got a date. I have some things scheduled but I'm going to break the appointments. I might as well start working on autonomy now. If you could leave the directions with my secretary, I'll see you at one-thirty sharp."

When the professor left, the One Minute Manager went to the window and stood looking out across the city. While he was standing quietly, his mind was moving a mile a minute. He reflected once again on his accomplishments as a manager over the years. He was proud of his record and his reputation, but this morning, more than ever before, he clearly realized that his success had had its price. His life was out of balance, to say the least.

"The professor has hit me at the right time," the One Minute Manager realized. "I'm excited about getting started on turning my life around."

AFTER lunch the next day, the One Minute Manager headed out to the university. He had met the president at a local Chamber of Commerce meeting the first week he was in town but hadn't spent any real time on the campus. He knew the university had grown from its early beginnings to become a significant institution with a variety of programs. Today the campus dominated one section of the city.

When the One Minute Manager entered the university gate, he stopped at the security booth to ask where he could park during his visit at the Lifestyle and Fitness Research Center.

"Park in Visitor Lot A," said the security guard. "It's straight ahead and then to the left."

As the One Minute Manager headed toward his suggested parking place, he smiled as he remembered hearing a university defined as "thousands of people gathered together around a common parking problem."

As he left his car and began to walk toward the Lifestyle and Fitness Research Center, the One Minute Manager wondered what it would be like to run a place as big as this; quite different, he imagined.

When he reached the professor's office, the secretary greeted him. "The professor is expecting you. Why don't you go right in."

"Thanks," said the One Minute Manager.

The professor jumped up immediately when he saw the One Minute Manager come through the door.

"Good to see you again. Hope you didn't have any trouble finding the place."

"Your directions were very clear."

"Let me show you around before we get down to work."

"I'd enjoy that," said the One Minute Manager. "I understand this place is only five years old."

As they walked around the facility, the One Minute Manager was really impressed. It had a twenty-five-meter lap pool; strength, flexibility, and exercise rooms; a gym with four basketball courts and a one-tenth mile track around them; six racquetball courts; and locker-room facilities for both men and women, which included saunas. There was a full-time fitness staff of four, which included the professor as director, a fitness and lifestyle counselor, a nutritionist and an exercise physiologist. There were also fitness-testing facilities, including two electric treadmills, a body-fat-measuring pool, and two counseling conference rooms. In addition, there were two beautiful classrooms with extensive audiovisual equipment.

The One Minute Manager could see how proud the professor was of this facility. "What an impressive operation this is," he said.

"Thanks," said the professor. "A lot of work and planning went into it. These facilities were a response to the increasing awareness of the impact of health on quality of life and productivity. More and more people like yourself are beginning to take a hard look at the kind of shape they are in and are starting to make changes in their lifestyle. To help you take a closer look at where you are now in terms of the four stress moderators and your total fitness, I'd like you to talk with Rose Greenberg, our fitness counselor."

When the One Minute Manager met Rose Greenberg, he could see she took fitness seriously. Greenberg was a slender woman who looked like the epitome of health.

Greenberg began by saying, "I understand you and the professor have talked about the relationship between productivity, health, and physical fitness."

"Yes, we have. I am ready to work on my tone. I can see how better tone can get my whole life back in balance. I'd like to become a healthy person again. But I think I've forgotten what that means."

"In order to help you know what it feels like to be healthy, let me ask you a series of questions. For each question, give yourself a one if you answer 'yes' and a zero if you answer 'no.'"

"Sounds intriguing. What are the questions?"

"Here they are," said Greenberg as she handed the One Minute Manager a card. "We call them The Professor's Dozen."

THE HEALTHY LIFESTYLE GUIDE*

The Professor's Dozen

1. I love my job. (Most of the time)
2. I use safety precautions like wearing a seat belt in moving vehicles.
3. I am within five pounds of my ideal weight.
4. I know three methods to reduce stress that do not include the use of drugs or alcohol.
5. I do not smoke.
6. I sleep six to eight hours each night and wake up refreshed.
7. I engage in regular physical activity at least three times per week. (Including sustained physical exertion for twenty to thirty minutes—for example, walking briskly, running, swimming, biking—plus strength and flexibility activities)
8. I have seven or fewer alcoholic drinks a week.
9. I know my blood pressure.
10. I follow sensible eating habits. (Eat breakfast every day; limit salt, sugar, and fats like butter, eggs, whole milk, breakfast meats, cheese, and red meat; and eat adequate fiber and few snacks.)
11. I have a good social support system.
12. I maintain a positive mental attitude.

---

*These items show up in the research studies conducted by the Health Management Research Center at the University of Michigan and in many studies conducted by others. Many of the factors are included in *Promoting Health, Preventing Disease: Objectives for the Nation,* Office of the Surgeon General, United States Department of Health and Human Services, Washington, D.C., 1994.

"THOSE are interesting statements," said the One Minute Manager as he began to put a one or a zero next to each. When he finished, he looked up.

"If you got ten or eleven points, we can stop our discussion now because you are doing most everything you should be doing."

"I'm afraid we can keep talking," smiled the One Minute Manager.

"What are your 'yes' items?"

"I love my job, I do not smoke, I have seven or fewer alcoholic drinks a week, I maintain a positive mental attitude, and for whatever it's worth, I eat breakfast every day. It's just the rest of the day that's a problem. I have a good social-support system, although I'm not sure I use it enough."

"So you could answer only four with a clear yes."

"I'm afraid so."

"What do you think most of your key people would score?" asked Greenberg.

"That's an interesting question," reflected the One Minute Manager, realizing he had never thought about the health of his key people. But if any of them was seriously disabled or killed, it would be very costly.

When the One Minute Manager, deep in thought, looked up, Greenberg was smiling. "That question was a real show stopper," said the One Minute Manager. "Unfortunately, I think my people would score about the same as I did."

"Were you surprised by any of the statements on the list?" asked Greenberg.

"Yes, several of them. 'Do you love your job?' That was surprising to me. But I would imagine that has implications for autonomy, connectedness, and perspective. Also, 'wearing seat belts,' but when I think about it, that makes sense, too. A lot fewer people would die in auto accidents if they had their seat belts on. Are there any other safety precautions that you would recommend?" wondered the One Minute Manager.

"Driving at a reasonable speed is one. It's amazing how that alone can reduce automobile deaths."

"Any other precautions?"

"Making sure you have smoke detectors that work well, both at work and at home. Accidents and death from fire are still a significant problem.

"I would recommend," continued Greenberg, "that you bend your knees when lifting things. Let your legs take the bulk of the strain from lifting rather than your back. Unfortunately, well over fifty percent of the adult population in our country has some kind of back problem. In addition, wearing hearing protection in high-noise environments and eye and skin protection in extremely bright or sunny conditions can be important, too."

"It sounds as if practicing safety precautions just involves using your head."

"That's it," said Greenberg. "Good old-fashioned common sense. Do you have any questions about other items on The Professor's Dozen?"

"Yes. What do you mean by strength and flexibility training activities?"

"A minimum strength exercise would be doing ten sit-ups and ten push-ups two to three times a week. Bringing your knees to your chest one at a time and holding for thirty seconds, and then both together four or five times, would be a minimum flexibility exercise. That would lessen the chance of back problems."

"So you think exercise is important."

"Absolutely, since exercise is the key to tone. In addition, to continue to improve in exercising, people must improve their lifestyle—reduce body weight, stop smoking, improve nutrition, get adequate sleep. When they do that, the results can be fantastic."

"Exercise is certainly something I am delinquent on and I know that it's not smart. One other thing comes to mind. You seem to suggest that drinking alcohol is OK."

"Within limits," said Greenberg. "No more than one drink a day."

"Could you skip drinks during the week and load up on Saturday?"

"I wouldn't recommend it unless you like headaches," smiled Greenberg.

"My own philosophy is to stay away from drinking. If you don't drink, we certainly do not suggest you start. Any other questions?"

"One final one. What do you mean by a positive mental attitude?"

"That you're basically an 'up person' and think life is a very special occasion and should be enjoyed," said Greenberg.

"How do you develop a positive mental attitude?"

"It's just like everything else. It's a choice. Some people just choose to live life harder than others. You can give them a compliment and they will discount it and wonder what you are up to. You can say, 'It's a beautiful day,' and they will respond with, 'Yes, but I hear it's going to be a lousy day tomorrow.' If something goes wrong they are devastated and take a long time to rally."

"So having a positive mental attitude is a choice, too, just like smoking or exercising."

"Definitely," said Greenberg. "We can't always control what happens in our lives—things will go well, things will go poorly—but what we can control is our response to those events. I always loved what Eleanor Roosevelt said: 'No one can make you feel inferior without your permission.'"

"I would imagine a good sense of humor would help here."

"Particularly if you can laugh at yourself."

"That takes a solid self-image, doesn't it?"

"It certainly does," said Greenberg. "And a good sense of connectedness. We need family, friends, co-workers, and even bosses we can talk to and laugh with when things happen that seem out of our control. Reaching out to them can sometimes help us maintain a positive attitude."

"Were you surprised by anything that wasn't on the list?" said Greenberg.

"Yes, I thought coffee consumption and environmental and occupational hazards would be on the list."

"I can see that you are well read on a variety of subjects. The effect of coffee consumption is very individual. That is, some people are affected by two cups while others can apparently drink much more than that. Some people have gone to decaffeinated coffee with good results. Your reference to environmental and occupational hazards is extremely important and has to be examined on a location to location basis. The hazards vary from one workplace to another."

"What about dental care? That's certainly a life choice."

"That's for sure," said Greenberg. "A dentist friend of mine told me recently, 'You don't have to brush and floss your teeth—only the ones you want to keep.'"

"That's funny but true," smiled the One Minute Manager. "Before I talked to the professor last week, I would have been surprised at the questions about knowing how to reduce stress and knowing your blood pressure. How did you come up with that list of statements and why?"

"LET me answer the 'why' question first," said Greenberg.

"That sounds fair."

"Today we are in the midst of a medical revolution. People are no longer dying from infectious diseases like scarlet fever, tuberculosis, and the like."

"I guess medical research and public-health efforts have taken care of those."

"That's right. What people are dying from today are chronic diseases we bring on ourselves."

"You mean the good life is killing us," smiled the One Minute Manager.

"Precisely. In fact, only a small percentage of what people are getting sick and dying from today can be controlled by the medical profession. By far the largest percentage has to do with the way one lives."

"Things really have changed, haven't they? In the old days when you got sick, you could just be miserable in peace. But nowadays, everyone is asking you to figure out what you did to cause it."

"That's true," said Greenberg. "Today when you get sick, rather than being offered chicken soup, you're apt to get a healing tape."

"A healing tape?"

"That's a cassette tape program that gives you some exercises to do to get your mind working to heal yourself."

"I guess the relationship between mind and body is becoming clearer and clearer, isn't it?"

"Yes, and that gets us back to our statements. You will notice that every one of them involves a personal choice from you."

"I understand what you are getting at now. The difference between a 'yes' and a 'no' answer has little to do with family history, heredity, or the like. The difference is choice. That's what autonomy is all about, isn't it?"

"That's important for you to realize," said Greenberg. "I'll have to praise the professor. He must have done a super job explaining about the stress moderators. Autonomy is exactly that—all about the power to choose how you will live. I can't say it enough. . . .

Today health,
more than ever
before,
is the outcome
of the way
you choose to
lead your life.

"So you can change any of your 'no' answers to 'yes' answers by personal choice," said the One Minute Manager.

"Precisely. And the way you choose to live your life determines where you find yourself on a wellness continuum." With that, Greenberg handed the One Minute Manager a sheet of paper with a drawing of a lifestyle scale.

LIFESTYLE SCALE

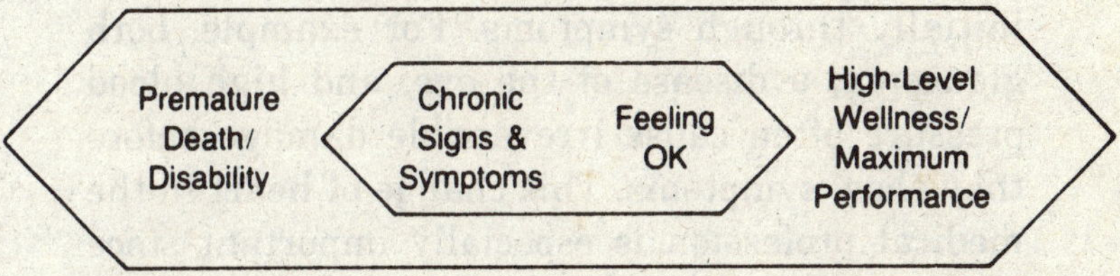

When the One Minute Manager finished looking over the lifestyle scale, Greenberg continued, "It used to be that we thought of people as either sick and in the hospital or healthy and not in the hospital. In the past thirty years we have changed our minds and now realize that there is a whole continuum of health. Of course, as you can see, on one end is premature death and on the other end is high-level wellness—a state of well-being where one is optimizing his or her life energy and performance."

"If you reach high-level wellness, I would imagine your tone would be in great shape and you would undoubtedly be stress resistant."

"You sure would be. The medical profession has traditionally been trained to deal with those people with signs and symptoms of premature death or disability. However, in recent years, some doctors have become interested in evaluating risk factors like age, sex, race, family history, and lifestyle habits, as well as including procedures in their physical examinations that look hard for problems that give no warning initially through symptoms. For example, both glaucoma, a disease of the eye, and high blood pressure often cause irreversible damage before they show symptoms. This change of heart in the medical profession is especially important since most people fall in the middle of the continuum between 'feeling OK' and 'chronic signs and symptoms.' To reach the state of maximum performance, people need not only knowledge and a positive attitude about healthy life habits, but a commitment to behave in healthy, productive ways. Your answers to The Professor's Dozen questions should have given you a good idea of where you fall on this health continuum."

"It looks as if I am in between 'chronic signs and symptoms' and 'feeling OK.' I certainly have a long way to go."

"How many people do you know who would rationally choose to move to the left on the scale?"

"THAT seems pretty obvious. No one."

"That certainly makes sense," said Greenberg, "yet we know many people are not choosing to follow a healthy and productive lifestyle. By the choices they are making, they are moving themselves toward the left side of the scale. Since we now know a lot about how healthy and productive people live, the message is clear that you can choose to follow healthy habits as described in The Professor's Dozen. In fact, as an organization you can now choose to provide an atmosphere at the work site that will help people make wise lifestyle choices."

"Can you imagine what it would be like if everyone chose to move to the right of the scale?"

"Sure. There would be tremendous energy that could potentially propel people to all kinds of record performances."

"Might we eventually put the medical profession out of business and decrease our health costs to a minimum?"

"A movement in that direction is certainly possible, but there will always be a need for the medical profession to participate in screening and evaluating risk factors, as well as treating people who do become ill. While we believe in self-responsibility, we all realize there are occasions in life that are beyond our control. The secret is to recognize which factors are under our control and respond to them."

"IF I worked on my lifestyle and was able to change all my 'no' answers to 'yes' answers, would I live longer?" wondered the One Minute Manager.

"That's the big picture. If you follow a healthy lifestyle, our research, and the work of many others, indicate that you will not only have a lesser chance of getting sick or dying prematurely but you will also have a higher-quality and more productive life. I could be more specific about your situation if you would fill out a Health Risk Appraisal."

"A what?" said the One Minute Manager.

"A Health Risk Appraisal. We call it the HRA," said Greenberg as she pulled a form from her briefcase and handed it to the One Minute Manager. "The HRA is a short questionnaire that will take you about ten minutes to complete. If you are honest, the analysis of your answers to the HRA will provide important information on your present and future physical health status."

"Why do you say if I am honest?"

"Unfortunately, people often cheat at solitaire," smiled Greenberg. "That's the problem with self-reported questionnaires. We are depending on your willingness to be honest. And yet we know that some people try to fool themselves as well as us when it comes to analyzing their own lifestyles. Recently I was working with a group of twenty-five top managers and I asked, 'How many of you smoke?' Only six people answered yes and then at lunch I counted eight smokers."

"That's amazing," said the One Minute Manager. "I want to assure you that if the analysis of any questions you ask me can be helpful to me, you can count on my answers' being truthful."

"I figured that would be your reaction. Your responses to the questions on the HRA can be used to estimate your health risk. The questions are designed to show how your present lifestyle affects your chances of avoiding the most common causes of illness (heart disease, lung cancer, stroke, cirrhosis of the liver, motor-vehicle accidents, other cancers) for a person of your age, race, and sex. Once your health risk has been assessed, you will know the probability of your current lifestyle's either increasing or decreasing your chances of illness or premature death."

"So you'll be able to tell me fairly accurately what the statistics show about my risk of getting sick or dying prematurely and how they could change if I did some things like lose weight."

"You've got it," said Greenberg. "I'll be able to tell you your appraised age compared to your actual age. This number indicates whether your health risk is equal to that of an older individual or whether your risk is less than or equal to that of individuals of the same age, sex, and race. And we'll be able to find out whether you fit the normal pattern," smiled Greenberg as she wrote a saying on a note pad she was using:

In early life, people give up their health to gain wealth . . .

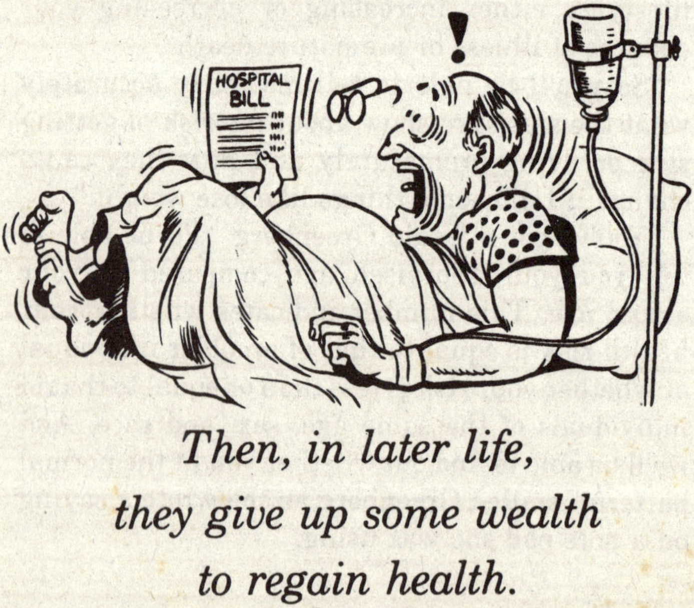

Then, in later life, they give up some wealth to regain health.

"You've aroused my curiosity," said the One Minute Manager. "I'm ready to fill out the HRA."

"Great," said Greenberg. "Why don't you fill it out at my desk and I'll go down the hall and find the professor. I know he wants to talk with you after you complete the HRA.

As she left the room, the One Minute Manager went to Greenberg's desk and began filling out the HRA. As he worked his way through the questions on the first page, a number of things came to mind. He noticed that besides asking about age, sex, and race, there were items about health habits and the stress moderators he had been discussing with Greenberg and the professor.

As the One Minute Manager read the questions directed toward family background, he thought about his dad who had died of a heart attack shortly after he had retired. While his mom was still alive, she had some diabetes in her family.

"I just haven't taken the time out to have an annual physical exam," he thought to himself as he got to the questions about rectal exam, blood pressure, and cholesterol level. He didn't even know if he had any problems in those areas.

As the One Minute Manager answered the questions about the strength of social ties, he thought, "I have a wonderful family and friends, but I don't always take the time with them that I should."

The final page of the HRA asked questions about stress and personal background and had some special questions for women. As he read the stress questions, the One Minute Manager once again realized the potential danger in his present situation. "The stress I am experiencing, combined with my weight problem and lack of exercise, could really be a potential killer," he thought to himself.

Just as he completed the questionnaire, the One Minute Manager heard the professor and Greenberg at the door. The One Minute Manager looked up with a smile as they entered. "This was very interesting. I'm anxious to find out what it all means," he said as he handed his questionnaire to the professor.

"We'll keep your questionnaire with us," said the professor, "and have it scored by computer. Then I can come over to your office tomorrow afternoon and give you some feedback."

"That's a deal," said the One Minute Manager as he stood up and said good-bye to the professor and Greenberg. "Thanks for your help, Rose, and I'll see you tomorrow afternoon, Professor."

"Until tomorrow," smiled the professor. "Remember, the way you live your life does not have to be hazardous to your health."

WHEN the professor arrived at the One Minute Manager's office the next afternoon, he was greeted with a smile. "Do you have good news or bad news?"

"I have 'starting place' news. Today is the first day of the rest of your life."

As soon as they sat down, the professor began. "Before I give you your HRA feedback, let me make some big-picture statements. The data from your HRA suggests that the way you are living gives you a risk of dying in the next ten years equal to that of a fifty-year-old person of the same sex and race. Since you are only forty-five years old, that should get your attention."

"If I followed your recommendations, how much of an impact could I have?"

"You could have the health risk of a forty-two-year-old person—a difference of eight years. While this news is bad enough, the difference in potential years lost would increase significantly as you got older if you made no lifestyle changes."

"I think you have convinced me that there are big risks in the way I have been living."

"It's good you are finding this out now while you can still do something about it." With that, the professor handed the One Minute Manager his computer-tabulated HRA feedback. "Why don't you read this and we can talk further."

When the One Minute Manager finished reading his feedback, he and the professor talked for over half an hour about the implications of the findings. This discussion focused on the need for the One Minute Manager to begin a regular exercise and healthy eating program.

"Since smoking and drinking are not a problem for you, sticking to a regular exercise and healthy eating program are the keys to bringing all your lifestyle habits in line, including returning some balance to your life," insisted the professor.

"I'm convinced of that now," said the One Minute Manager. "If I can get my tone back in shape, increased autonomy, better perspective, and improved connectedness will not be far behind."

"Believing that is an important step."

"Great. What else do I need to do to get started on a healthier lifestyle?"

"Since you are over forty and haven't been on an exercise program, I would strongly recommend you first have a complete physical examination. In fact, I would make that a part of your routine every couple of years now. Once you have done that, we can talk about the specifics of your program."

"That makes sense," said the One Minute Manager. "I'm just anxious to talk about the specifics of what I need to do so I can get started."

"To be honest with you," said the professor, "I'm not as worried about the specifics because I'm convinced that people really know at a commonsense level what intelligent eating is all about and what an acceptable exercise program should involve. The hard part is sticking to whatever you decide to do. In other words, it's easier said than done. So after you get a physical examination, I'd like you to learn what you have to do to change your behavior. Then we can get into the specifics of the program."

"So I have to change my behavior. I knew reality would come into the picture sometime. Because I try to get people to manage differently, I know changing behavior is not easy."

"It's all about keeping your commitments," said the professor. "People say diets don't work. Diets work fine. It's people who don't work. They break their agreements with themselves."

"So the road to hell is paved with good intentions."

"Precisely," said the professor. "Since that is true, I'd like to meet with you next Wednesday at Tech, Inc., on McGraw Street at one P.M. I've made an appointment for you next Monday afternoon with the medical doctor who does all of our physical exams. We work with him because he is not only interested in treating signs and symptoms of illness but also in examining risk factors and the impact of lifestyle."

"You think of everything, don't you," smiled the One Minute Manager.

"I try to. The reason I want us to meet at Tech, Inc., is twofold. First of all, Larry Armstrong, the president, is really into health promotion. He thinks it's almost a must for fast-growing high-tech companies. I want you to see how Larry has taken the concept of a healthy lifestyle beyond himself into this company. You might want to think about doing that down the road. Second, one of his key people, Leonard Hawkins, has done extensive training with us and is now teaching health-promotion classes to their people. I called Larry and he said they will be holding their 'behavior change' class on Wednesday afternoon. I'd love for you to sit in on that session. It will put into perspective what it will take to really act on your good intentions."

"Sounds interesting," said the One Minute Manager as he shook hands with the professor. "See you on Wednesday."

When the One Minute Manager left work later that afternoon he drove straight home. He told Alice about his discussions with the professor, and she was anxious to hear what he had learned from his HRA.

Alice was happy to hear his enthusiasm for getting started on an exercise and weight-loss program. So were his teenage children. Everyone supported the idea that this was "the year of the body."

When the One Minute Manager went for his physical examination on Monday afternoon, the doctor reinforced everything Rose Greenberg and the professor had said, and added one comment: "You have a fantastic heart surrounded by fifty pounds of fat."

While his blood pressure was not a problem now (135/85), the doctor warned the One Minute Manager that it was something he would soon have to watch if he did not change his ways. He suggested that the One Minute Manager start a healthy eating program and begin a supervised exercise program. But because he was a former jock, he should beware of overdoing it at first. The last words he said to the One Minute Manager were, "Remember, the motto of your training program should be . . .

Train . . .
don't
strain

WEDNESDAY afternoon came before the One Minute Manager knew it. After a light lunch he headed over to Tech, Inc. He had heard of the company and had seen Larry Armstrong at a couple of civic affairs, but he did not know him personally. He did know that Armstrong was founder of the company and had built it from nothing to over $100 million in gross sales in less than seven years.

When the One Minute Manager got to Larry Armstrong's office, the professor was waiting for him. After greeting each other, they headed into Armstrong's office at the suggestion of his secretary. They found it spacious and beautifully furnished. Armstrong was standing staring out the window overlooking the plant grounds. As he turned, the One Minute Manager thought to himself, "Another obnoxiously in-shape person."

"Nice to see you," said Armstrong when the professor introduced him to the One Minute Manager. "The professor tells me you're interested in health and fitness."

"Yes, I am, Mr. Armstrong," said the One Minute Manager. "I have been really excited about my meetings with the professor and Rose Greenberg and what I learned about my health risk. I wanted to get started on improving my own lifestyle and they suggested a good way to start would be to talk to you, see what you are doing here, and sit in on one of your sessions this afternoon."

"I think he's all thawed out and ready for change," said the professor to Armstrong, "and I thought Leonard's session on behavior change would be extremely helpful."

"Call me Larry," said Armstrong to the One Minute Manager with a warm smile. "I'm happy to tell you what we are doing here. We have about fifteen minutes before Leonard's session starts, so why don't you sit down?"

After getting settled, the One Minute Manager began, "Larry, I understand you have taken the professor's lifestyle ideas beyond just yourself and implemented an entire health-promotion program in your company. Why? What sold you on the concept so much?"

"Two things," said Armstrong. "The logic and the facts."

"The logic?" wondered the One Minute Manager.

"Yes," said Armstrong. "Let me ask you several questions. First of all, do you think a healthier person is a better employee?"

"Of course I do."

"If you have better employees, will you have a more productive organization?"

"Sure you will. They would go hand in hand."

"Would you agree then," asked Armstrong, "that if you have healthier employees, you will have a more productive organization?"

"I think your logic is sound, but I'd like to see that written down."

"Sure," said Armstrong. "Let me sketch it out."

IF HEALTHIER PEOPLE
are
BETTER
EMPLOYEES

AND BETTER
EMPLOYEES
provide
GAINS FOR THE
ORGANIZATION

THEN HEALTHIER PEOPLE
provide
GAINS FOR THE
ORGANIZATION

"THAT makes sense," said the One Minute Manager. "I buy the logic. Tell me about the facts."

"They speak for themselves," said Armstrong as he showed the One Minute Manager an employees' "Guide to Management and Quality of Work Programs" in their company. Armstrong had opened the guide to the section entitled "The Problem: Concern for People and Health Care Costs."

The facts popped out at the One Minute Manager as he looked at the guide.

THE FACTS*

- Illness-related costs to employers are high: Industry pays nearly 30 percent of a national health-care bill that now exceeds $1 trillion per year.

- Corporate health expenses range from $1,200 to $6,000 per employee per year, averaging $2,400. These costs have been rising at twice the rate of general inflation.

- U. S. business spends every year an estimated $40 billion in workers' compensation and loses untold billions in reduced productivity because of over 500 million worker days lost to illness and injury.

- Health-care costs consume as much as $1 out of every $9 the average worker earns.

- It is reported that the total cost of replacement of a top executive of a major corporation due to premature mortality is $1.5 million.

- A *Fortune* 500 company estimated the cost of mid- to lower-level-management turnover at $8,500 per occurence, clerical turnover at $4,000. The strong association between high turnover rates and ill health is said to be clear.

- In one of our midwestern states, it was reported that heart disease costs employers every year:

  One million lost workdays
  $14 million in replacement costs
  $162 million in disability payments
  $900 million estimated total for direct and productivity costs
  A single heart attack survived costs an employer on the average $21,551.

- Smoking-related illness, poor diet and lack of exercise, and alcoholism account for 800,000 deaths in the United States every year.

- Absenteeism is 40 percent greater in smokers, generating millions of lost workdays per year.

*These facts have been widespread in the health-care-cost literature over the last several years.

"THOSE are staggering facts," said the One Minute Manager.

"They sold me," said Armstrong.

"How long have you been operating your quality-of-life programs?" wondered the One Minute Manager.

"For three years now," said Armstrong. "We run educational classes here but our people use the facilities at the university, the YMCA and YWCA, health clubs, and local recreation centers for their exercising. We do have showers, though, if people want to jog during lunch hour or before or after work. Someday I hope to have an entire building devoted to health promotion, the way the professor has with the Lifestyle and Fitness Research Center."

"How would you justify that kind of expenditure?" asked the One Minute Manager.

"I can already justify it," said Armstrong. "It's a matter of getting the land nearby and taking the time to plan it. Let me give you some examples of what has happened since I got behind health promotion in this company."

THE BENEFITS*

- Our health-care expenditures are now averaging 80 percent of those experienced before the introduction of our exercise, smoking cessation, nutrition, and blood-pressure-control programs.

- Three years into the program, our employees are using one-fifth fewer sick-leave days.

- Our absenteeism rate is down more than 15 percent.

- Our quality-of-life programs have been a tangible way to demonstrate to our employees that "the company cares about you" and the results have been improved morale and commitment to the organization, better communication among employees, and a far lower turnover rate than ever before—a real win-win situation.

- We have found that our employees are now making more appropriate use of the health system. They are going for help for the right reasons at the right time.

- We estimate returns averaging $136 for every $100 invested in our quality-of-life programs and expect the return rate to get even better five to seven years into the program.

- Of all our health-care cost-containment strategies, this program has the highest employee support.

*These benefits are examples of actual company experiences identified by the Health Management Research Center at the University of Michigan.

"THOSE results are almost too good to believe," said the One Minute Manager.

"I agree," said Armstrong. "It took tremendous effort from all our employees. There has been a lot of behavior change going on. I should also mention that we are beginning to examine the impact of various aspects of the company on employee wellness, including such things as: work and safety habits, environmental factors such as air flow and temperature, and organizational matters like structure, performance-review procedures, and the elements of job and supervisor satisfaction and dissatisfaction. We are finding that this analysis has led us to more and better communication with our people, as well as to the development of improved management-training programs. We have a long way to go in this area, but our efforts have again demonstrated our long-term commitment to our employees and to the health of the organization. It's a real change effort."

"Talking about that," said the professor, "isn't it about time for your class on behavior change to start?"

"You're right," said Armstrong as he got to his feet and headed for the door. The One Minute Manager and the professor had to move quickly to keep up with him. Armstrong smiled as he passed his secretary and said, "We'll be back in about an hour."

As they headed upstairs, Armstrong told them that they were going to a session for new managers, all of whom knew the characteristics of a healthy lifestyle, had taken the HRA, and had had a complete physical examination. Each of them was about to launch his or her own individual wellness program based on the recommendations from the HRA and the physical examination.

"The person doing the training is Leonard Hawkins, one of our experienced managers," said Armstrong.

"He isn't a trainer?" asked the One Minute Manager.

"He is now, but not by profession," said Armstrong. "In fact, Leonard is a mechanical engineer by trade. The professor and his staff have trained several of our people to present the various health-promotion sessions. This session concludes our ten-session series for these managers."

"What are the topics of these sessions besides behavior change?" wondered the One Minute Manager.

"They also have sessions on lifestyle, heart disease and stroke, fitness and exercise, alcohol abuse, giving up smoking, safety and environmental precautions, nutrition and eating habits, cancer, and programs on managing stress and time," said Armstrong.

"All these sessions are related to the lifestyle choices and behavior we know influence where a person falls on the wellness continuum."

"Without a high quality of life," Armstrong continued, "we feel it is difficult to be effective in training any of our employees in job skills or in improving work-site efficiency. As a result, all these topics are integrated into our employee training programs, including career planning and leadership workshops. We think all these topics are part of the same overall goal—developing our people to become all they can become. If everyone has this goal, we will certainly be more successful as a company."

The One Minute Manager was trying to take in what Armstrong was saying as they entered the back of the seminar room. There were about twenty young managers in the session. Leonard Hawkins was up front and seemed to be leading into an exercise.

"Our timing was perfect," said Armstrong as they sat down.

"Does anyone have any more questions about the characteristics of a healthy lifestyle?" asked Hawkins. There was silence throughout the room. A few people shook their heads "no."

"OK. If there are no questions, let me ask one," said Hawkins. "How many of you feel good about what you have learned and intend to do something to change your present lifestyle?"

Everybody's hand went up.

"So you all know what it takes to lead a healthy lifestyle," said Hawkins, "and seem to have *positive feelings* about changing unhealthy habits. Let me get you involved in an exercise that may give you some insights into how to put your knowledge and attitudes into practice. Everyone stand up and find yourself a learning partner."

When a man raised his hand and said he did not have a partner, Hawkins signaled the One Minute Manager to join the exercise, which he did.

"All right, now that everybody has a partner," shouted out Hawkins, "I want you to face your partner and take a minute of silence to observe the physical characteristics of your partner—his or her clothes, face, body. But no talking. Just observe your partner."

Quiet laughter spread throughout the room and even a murmur of voices.

"No talking," reminded Hawkins. "Just observe your partner."

An uncomfortable feeling came over the One Minute Manager. "Here I am standing in front of this stranger and I'm asked to stare at him," he thought. He didn't know where to put his eyes and neither did the other man. "What is Hawkins up to?" he wondered. This certainly felt like a "touchy-feely" game. It was the longest minute he could ever recall.

"OK," said Hawkins. "The minute is up. Now turn your back on your partner so you can't see each other."

The One Minute Manager and his partner turned around.

"What I want you to do now that you have your back to your partner is to make five physical changes in your appearance so when you turn around your partner will see five things that are different about the way you look."

The One Minute Manager was still confused by the experience, but he slowly began to make some changes in his appearance. He changed his watch from his left wrist to his right wrist. He took off his tie. As he looked around the room, the faces of the other participants suggested confusion too.

"When you have finished making your changes, check with your partner. When you have both made your five changes, turn around and try to identify each other's changes."

When the One Minute Manager turned around, he quickly saw his partner had taken off his glasses and removed his jacket. "Those are two changes," he thought. "Maybe this is not going to be as hard as I thought."

When they had finished guessing each other's changes, Hawkins broke in again. "Now turn your backs on each other again." As people finished turning around, Hawkins shouted out, "You made five changes in your physical appearance last time. This time I want you to make ten more changes."

The whole room went into an uproar. "Ten more changes! You've got to be crazy," shouted one man.

"Can we change our five back?" questioned another.

"Changing back your original five doesn't count," clarified Hawkins. "You need ten new changes—fifteen altogether."

People still shouted out more questions. Hawkins calmly repeated, "Ten new changes."

The One Minute Manager thought to himself, "This is crazy. I just don't have enough to take off or change. Pretty soon this is going to be strip poker." He began to feel uncomfortable again.

As he looked around the room he saw that a number of people had stopped trying. They were just standing there waiting for the exercise to be over.

One fellow was really getting into it, though, and was becoming creative, doing such things as putting paper in his ears and using his belt as a tie. He made the One Minute Manager laugh and motivated him to begin to think what he could do. The whole exercise still did not make any sense to him but he thought he'd try anyway. "There must be some point to this," he thought.

After he had made his seventh change, the One Minute Manager heard Hawkins say, "When you have made your ten changes, check with your partner. When you have both finished making your changes, turn around and see if you can see the new changes."

The One Minute Manager's partner indicated he had finished his changes. Although the Manager had only made seven changes, he decided he couldn't think of any more so he turned around to face his partner. He immediately began to see some of his partner's changes. He had parted his hair differently, taken off his shoes, and made several other obvious alterations. The One Minute Manager began to relax again.

After they had finished guessing, Hawkins told everyone to sit down.

"All right. Some of you are probably asking yourself if I have lost my mind." Many of the participants smiled and nodded agreement.

"Well, I haven't lost my mind," continued Hawkins. "Knowing about the characteristics of a healthy lifestyle and feeling positive about trying to change some of your present behavior are very important steps to becoming healthier. But they are only the beginning. The toughest step is to take new knowledge and attitudes and begin to behave differently. That involves real change. That's what this exercise was all about—CHANGE."

"I knew it was about something," laughed one of the participants. "I just couldn't figure out what."

"Well, let's take a look at it," said Hawkins. "First of all, when I said 'No talking for a minute and just observe the physical characteristics of your partner,' what were some of the feelings you were having? Just shout them out and I'll write them on the blackboard."

Uncomfortable

Awkward

Didn't know where to put my eyes

Silly

Self-conscious

The participants had no trouble identifying their feelings.

Why?

Embarrassed

A minute is a long period of time

"All right," intervened Hawkins. "We could go on and try to identify more feelings, but I think we have enough. Let's look at them. Those feelings you had when you were asked to do something you are not used to doing—look at someone while that person is looking at you—are the same feelings people have whenever you ask them to do something different. They feel uncomfortable, awkward, silly, self-conscious, and embarrassed—all those feelings."

"That's the truth, isn't it?" thought the One Minute Manager.

"Those are the same feelings you will have the first time you begin to walk or jog in your neighborhood or follow any of our recommendations," continued Hawkins.

"I was worried about that," said a woman, "particularly having my neighbors see me out exercising."

"I was beginning to wonder what I'd do at parties if I couldn't smoke," said a young man.

"While all the healthy life habits make sense," said Hawkins, "when it comes to doing them, that may be a different story."

"Will those feelings of awkwardness ever change?" asked a participant.

"Sure they will," said Hawkins, "but it will take time and support from others. The important thing is not to put yourself down for having those feelings. They are very natural."

"I didn't have any problem with the staring part," said a woman manager. "I started to feel uncomfortable when you told us to make changes."

"Let's look at that," said Hawkins. "When I asked you to make some changes in your physical appearance, you all did some interesting things that have a lot to say about the difficulty of change."

"I bet we did," laughed one of the managers.

"First of all, everyone seemed to be trying to take something off. Almost no one tried to put something on.

"And those of you who stopped participating in the exercise were grumbling something like 'I just didn't wear enough clothes today,'" smiled Hawkins.

"I get it," said a woman. "When you ask someone to do something differently, the first thing they think is 'What do I have to give up?'"

"Precisely. Have you ever heard anyone at the beginning of a change effort talking about what they are going to gain from the change?"

"Very seldom," commented another manager. "It's always what we're going to lose."

"As a result," continued Hawkins, "we need to legitimize those feelings of loss. If you don't, you will never be able to appreciate what you will gain from the change. Let's talk about some of the things you will lose if you start to live a healthy lifestyle."

"Time!" shouted out a manager. "Exercising takes time."

"That's the number-one concern of most people," interjected Hawkins.

"Desserts," smiled another.

"A cigarette after a meal," suggested someone else. "That's going to be awful."

"Freedom to do whatever I want to do," said a woman. "I'm going to have to show self-control."

"Those are not going to be easy, are they?" said Hawkins. "How did you feel about talking about them?"

"I feel much better about things when I talk about them," said a manager. "Otherwise, I continue to think about them."

"Exactly," said Hawkins. "Now we can more easily talk about what we will gain. What are your thoughts on the positive side?"

"Feeling good about myself. Not putting myself down for having no willpower."

"Being able to get a sense of accomplishment."

"Not being out of breath all the time."

"Probably living longer. Life is so wonderful it would be silly to end it early."

"Feeling good about yourself, a sense of accomplishment, not being out of breath, living longer—those sound pretty good to me," said Hawkins.

"How about being more productive?" asked a woman manager. "Having more energy would permit us to work harder but enjoy it more. That would not be a bad gain, would it?"

"All those gains sound great," said Hawkins. "This is the kind of conversation I recommend you have with your family, friends, co-workers, and boss—anyone who can support your change effort and whose you can support. It will make a big difference in actually changing your lifestyle."

"I noticed that almost no one helped anyone else during the exercise," said a manager.

"Good point," said Hawkins. "It's interesting that whenever a change is implemented, even if the entire organization, or everyone in your family, is going through it together, everyone feels alone. As you had your backs to your partners and were making your changes, you were facing a bunch of other people who had their backs to their partners and were doing the same thing. Did I tell you that you couldn't help each other?"

"He certainly did not," thought the One Minute Manager as all the participants shook their heads.

"And yet, even though you were facing others who were going through the same change situation," continued Hawkins, "almost no one helped someone else. You were trying to make the changes all by yourselves."

"Is that typical?" asked a manager.

"Very," said Hawkins. "That's why we feel so strongly that to really change your lifestyle you have to share your goals with everyone who can support your effort—both at work and at home. You cannot make these changes all by yourself. It is important to remember:

To

keep on track,

most of us

need the support

of

the people

who care

for us.

"That's for sure!" laughed a manager. "If I'm going to lose the weight I need to lose, my kids cannot keep all those cookies and treats all over the house."

"How right you are," said Hawkins. "That would be a disaster. And one last thing—what happened when you all thought the exercise was over?"

"We all changed back to where we were before," said a manager. "We got dressed again—even if we felt more comfortable with the new changes."

"Good observation," said Hawkins. "After a change is started, if the pressure is taken off, people will return to old behaviors. For example, people lose weight when they diet but it is often only short-term. If they don't stay on some maintenance program, they will soon go off the diet and return to their former eating behavior. When that happens, their weight returns to the previous level. Only if there is a true behavior change in their eating patterns will body weight remain at the lower level."

"That's really interesting," thought the One Minute Manager. "Hawkins certainly has made some good points from this exercise."

"The first level of change is *knowledge*, continued Hawkins. "That is the easiest and least time-consuming change to make. Just reading a diet book or listening to me or getting a membership to a health club can change your knowledge about a healthy lifestyle. I think we have done that."

"What's the difference between knowledge and attitude?" asked one manager.

"An *attitude* is harder to change than knowledge. It is an emotionally charged bit of knowledge. Now you feel positive or negative about something you know. As we discussed earlier, my sense is that most of you have very positive feelings toward improving your lifestyles."

"Are attitudes really more difficult to change than knowledge?"

"Yes," said Hawkins. "It's the old 'yes, but' trick. That's when you say, 'I know what you're saying, *but* I'm not going to change my opinion.'"

"What about *behavior*?" asked a woman. "Isn't it easier to change behavior than attitudes?"

"Only if I use force," said Hawkins. "If I were your boss and said, 'Do this or you're fired,' I'm sure I could get you to do something before you had a positive attitude about it."

"But unless you are using force," said a manager, "you would argue that it is easier to change attitudes than behavior."

"Yes," said Hawkins. "Let me give you an example. Take smoking. How many of you have smoking as one of your lifestyle problems?"

Ten people raised their hands.

"OK," said Hawkins. "Of you ten smokers, how many of you know smoking is no good for you?"

Again, ten hands went up.

"So all of you who smoke have knowledge about the potential health detriments of smoking," said Hawkins. "How many of you who smoke have a positive attitude toward giving it up if you could do it easily?"

This time only seven people raised their hands.

"I see by the reduction in hands," said Hawkins, "that some of you have dug in your heels and don't care that smoking is no good for you. I actually feel bad for you smokers because everyone is always picking on you. I have never heard anybody say to an overweight person, 'Stop eating. You are taking up my space.'"

Everyone got a good chuckle out of that comment.

"I sure want to give up smoking," said a man, "but I've been smoking for fifteen years and it's murder to quit, particularly after meals."

"How right you are," said Hawkins. "The same applies to those of us who have eating problems. I don't smoke, but when I got into this wellness program, I was about twenty-five to thirty pounds overweight. Now, I knew that extra weight was not good for my heart and I had a positive attitude toward shedding those extra pounds, but it was tough, particularly when I grew up with a mother who thought there was something wrong with a meal if you didn't have a second helping. And if that wasn't bad enough, I used to fantasize about being locked in a Jewish delicatessen overnight."

"I know how you feel," laughed a heavyset manager. "I can smell a piece of cheesecake a mile away."

"That's for sure," smiled Hawkins. "So it is hard to change our eating behavior when there are temptations all around us. Behavior is much tougher to change than attitudes unless you are being forced to change. It's amazing how quickly people change their eating habits when they have a heart attack and realize that they may die if they don't shed some extra pounds."

"SO you're suggesting," interrupted a manager, "that taking our knowledge and positive attitudes about a healthy lifestyle and transferring those into actions and behavioral change will be easier said than done."

"Yes, I am," said Hawkins.

"It's going to be hard for me to stick to any program," said a woman, "and not quit and jump on the next program I read or hear about."

"How right you are," said Hawkins, pointing to a plaque on a wall.

Most people
spend all their time
looking for the next
diet or exercise program
AND
very little time
staying with the program
they just started

AFTER everyone had read the plaque and knowing nods had passed around the room, Hawkins continued. "But luckily you're not in this alone. As an organization we are committed to wellness and helping you win. That's why I will be working with you as a group or individually continuously for the next six to nine months. We're going to help you so that reverting back to old behavior will not be easy. We do not think training in lifestyle is just a fringe benefit—a nice little frill that we can give all our employees. Wellness is something we think can have a real impact not only on your life but on your performance and the performance of the total organization. We view our lifestyle program as an important part of the cost of doing business."

With that said, Hawkins looked toward the back of the room and said, "Larry, would you be willing to comment on the kind of involvement in our wellness programs we hope to get from them this year."

"Sure," said Armstrong as he headed toward the front of the room. "While our wellness program from this point on is voluntary, we hope the positive attitudes generated here will lead you to make some necessary changes in your lifestyle.

"I hope we don't get halfhearted participation from you in our wellness program, but real commitment. After all, it's only your life and the future of our company we're talking about," said Armstrong.

"That sounds like a good wrap-up to me," said Hawkins. "I'll be meeting with each of you individually over the next week."

As the group began to gather their things up and leave, the One Minute Manager watched Armstrong greet and interact with the managers. He thought to himself, "You don't see many top managers show that kind of interest in the training of new managers."

As the last manager left, Armstrong turned and beckoned to the One Minute Manager. "Come on over," he said. "I'd like you to meet Leonard Hawkins." As the One Minute Manager shook hands with Hawkins, he said, "Thanks so much for letting me sit in on your session. I found it most informative. I got some good insights into why changing your lifestyle is easier said than done and some things I need to do to make it happen."

"I'm glad the exercise helped," said Hawkins as he greeted the professor.

"Thanks, Leonard," said Armstrong. Turning to the One Minute Manager, he said, "Why don't you and the professor come down with me to my office. I imagine you want to get started."

"THAT I do," said the One Minute Manager. "Thanks again, Leonard. Hope to see you sometime soon."

"My pleasure," said Hawkins. "You're in good hands."

When they arrived at his office, Armstrong asked the One Minute Manager, "What was most helpful about the session?"

"I really relearned a number of things," said the One Minute Manager. "In particular, I was fascinated by how similar the difficulties of implementing a new management approach are to changing one's lifestyle. That means several things to me. First of all, changing your lifestyle is going to take a real personal *commitment*, second, it is *not* going to be *easy;* third, the *help* of others is *needed;* and finally, *organizational and family* support can be invaluable in *implementing change* as well as *preventing a quick return* to old behavior."

"It sounds as if you got the message. I think you're ready for the specifics," said the professor as he handed the One Minute Manager his own copy of the Healthy Lifestyle Guide—the lifestyle questions called The Professor's Dozen.

"Let me leave you two to your work," said Armstrong. "If I can be of any help, let me know."

"You can count on that," said the One Minute Manager as he shook hands with Armstrong. "Thanks for your time today."

As Armstrong left, the professor turned to the One Minute Manager and said, "You'll notice that I've checked off on your own 'Gets Fit' Healthy Lifestyle Guide six items that you already have under control. In addition to the original four, you could answer yes to when we first talked—loving your job, not smoking, moderate drinking, and a positive mental attitude—I also checked knowing your blood pressure and having a good social system. After your physical examination, I'm sure you know your blood pressure, don't you?"

"Yes, it's 135/85. It was good news to hear that it was not a problem yet."

"*Yet* is an important word to underline," smiled the professor. "I also checked 'I have a good social support system' because you indicated you had one but just weren't using it. After the change exercise with Leonard Hawkins, I would imagine you will start to use your potential supporters."

"That's for sure. You know, as I look at the list, I think I'm lucky not to have a smoking or drinking problem. I know a lot of people who couldn't say that, and they are having an agonizing time getting those two under control."

"You do deserve a praising," smiled the professor. "In fact, with six yes answers, you're halfway home to a healthy lifestyle. Let's look at the ones you still have to work on."

"Using seat belts in moving vehicles will be an easy one to do," suggested the One Minute Manager. "All I have to do is decide to do it."

"Precisely. It's easy to remember to wear your safety belts in an airplane because the flight attendants are always closely supervising you. But when you are all alone in the car, the only reminder is your commitment. Keeping stress under control and sleeping six to eight hours each night to wake up refreshed may both fall in line if you get into a regular exercise program.

"I would hope so," said the One Minute Manager. "What would be a good beginning exercise program?"

"I would start with walking or swimming."

"Since I'm not a swimmer, and in fact have always defined swimming as staying alive in the water," smiled the One Minute Manager, "I'll stick with walking."

"In that case I would recommend you walk briskly for twenty to thirty minutes four times a week. Don't worry about your time at first. But eventually, I would hope you could build up to covering two miles in thirty minutes. That would mean you were traveling at a fifteen-minute-mile pace. After you begin to get comfortable, you might want to mix it up with some jogging or bicycling. You get the old heart pumping a lot quicker with those. But remember what the doctor said: Train—Don't Strain."

"Some of my friends who are addicted to exercise like to get out at least six times a week. Is that too much?"

"That's all right as long as you remember that you need only three or four days a week to get good aerobic benefit out of your exercise. Anything more than that you are doing for some other reason than your tone—for example, for the mental benefits of almost daily taking some time to do something intrinsically valuable and noncompetitive. Or you may want to get yourself in better shape to compete in 10K races or some other athletic competition. But let's cross that bridge when we come to it. For now, let's start the brisk walks three or four times a week."

"What about flexibility and strength activity?"

"If you can get into an exercise class at your health club or YMCA, one that meets two or three times a week, they could help you get started on strength and flexibility. But a minimum I would suggest is ten sit-ups and ten push-ups, then bringing your knees to your chest one at a time and holding for thirty seconds, and then both together for the same amount of time. Remember, though, you might have to work up to those numbers."

"How about my weight?"

"At 5′ 11″ the charts say you should weigh between 175 and 185. That means you have to lose a minimum of 51 pounds from your present 236 pounds. That's no small order. But an eating program combined with your exercise program should permit you to do that in six months to a year."

"So you recommend the slow and steady approach."

"Absolutely," said the professor. "We're talking about real lifestyle change, not a quick fix."

"In terms of my eating," said the One Minute Manager, "you implied it was just common sense. Since I like to keep things simple, how about if I eat for breakfast mostly fruit and/or nonsugar cereals; for lunch, a light sandwich on whole wheat or rye bread or a salad with an oil and vinegar dressing; and for dinner, mainly fish or chicken and a salad or brown rice."

"That sounds right on," said the professor. "Remember, you don't have to eliminate sugar, salt, and fats like eggs, butter, whole milk, breakfast meat, cheese, and red meats completely. Moderation is the key. But try to keep their use to no more than twice a week. For snacks use celery, carrots, or fruit. And to keep the system flowing, drink at least six glasses of water a day."

The One Minute Manager started to laugh.

"What's so funny?"

"The water. I remember Johnny Carson once interviewed a diet expert who advocated drinking a lot of water and said he knew why people were losing so much weight on his diet. They were running to the bathroom all the time."

The professor and the One Minute Manager had a good laugh.

"I think you have a good plan," said the professor. "Do you have any questions, though?"

"NO," said the One Minute Manager. "Sounds good to me. All I have to do is get started. As Harry Truman used to say: 'The buck stops here.'"

"Let's keep in touch," said the professor as he got up and shook hands with the One Minute Manager.

"I certainly intend to do that. Thanks for heading me in the right direction."

On his way home the One Minute Manager stopped by a couple of health clubs, the YMCA, and the local hospital to see their facilities and talk to some of their staff about their health and fitness programs.

When he got home he shared his experiences with Alice and the children. Together with their help and support, he began to set up a strategy for his weight-loss and exercise program.

The first step the One Minute Manager took was to create two graphs to use in keeping a weekly record of his weight-loss and exercise frequency. His weight graph for the first three months looked like this:

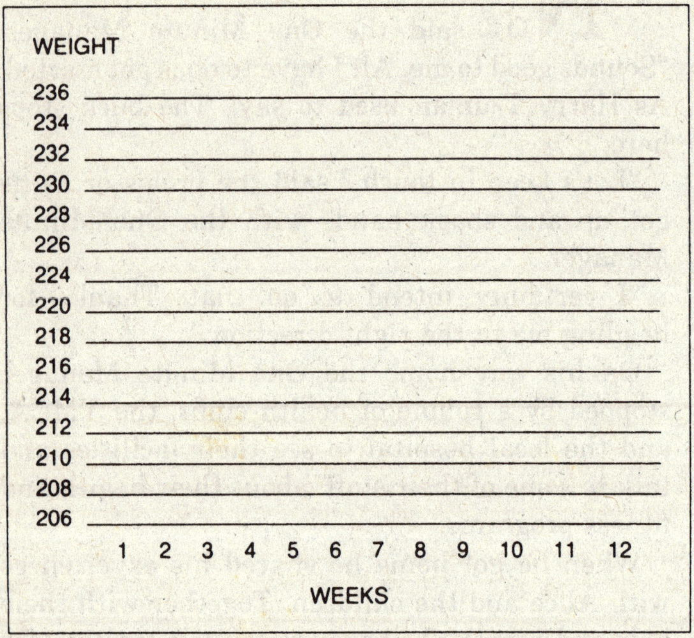

He set up similar weekly graphs to keep score of how many times each week he walked briskly for twenty to thirty minutes and how often he did some strength and flexibility exercises.

After further discussions with the doctor who had given him his physical exam and with the professor, the One Minute Manager set his goals in the two main areas of his "Healthy Lifestyle" program—weight loss and exercise. Although his long-range goal was to weigh between 175 and 185, his three-month goal was 210 pounds. That was a weight loss of about 2 pounds per week from his present 236 pounds.

To accomplish that, he would start gradually to work his way into the eating program that he had designed with the professor. The easiest change for him to make, he thought, would be eating mainly fruit or nonsugar cereals for breakfast.

He was not normally a big breakfast eater except when he would periodically pig out at one of the local restaurants and have sausage, eggs up, pancakes, and a couple of large glasses of milk. Lunch would be a little tougher because he loved a jumbo cheeseburger with an order of fries. Salads didn't turn him on, but he hoped he would really learn to like them and begin to taste the different types of lettuce and other rabbit food.

"Dinner will be the toughest," he admitted, since he often built his day up to a climax with a good steak or roast beef, a baked potato, a little vegetable, and all kinds of bread and butter—and, of course, dessert. The One Minute Manager had always worked hard for it and felt that he deserved it. The fact that his hard work was always from the neck up had never entered his mind.

In retrospect, the One Minute Manager was amazed that after a big dinner he usually was somehow ready for a little snack before bed—a piece of pie or a sandwich. Whichever one he chose it always seemed to go down more easily with a glass of milk.

What he hoped would help him the most was increasing his intake of water, particularly if he drank two glasses just before a meal. "That should kill some of my appetite," he thought. "And then I will be better able to ease into an appropriate meal." Within several weeks his goal was to have pretty well stopped adding salt, sugar, and butter at the table. Then he would cut eggs, whole milk, breakfast meats, cheese, and red meats to no more than two times a week each. He also wanted to reduce his moderate drinking to an occasional glass of wine. If he had more than that, his past history indicated that he would overeat.

As for exercise, the One Minute Manager's eventual goal was to walk briskly for forty-five minutes at least five times a week. If the weather prevented him from walking, he would ride on an exercise bike at the local health club he had decided to join. While five times a week sounded like a lot, and both the professor and the doctor had said, "Three times a week will do the trick," the One Minute Manager wanted to go for five days. As he learned from the professor, taking that time for himself to work on his tone could help him get back into balance the other stress moderators—autonomy, connectedness, and perspective.

To accomplish these goals, the One Minute Manager would start off by walking for ten to twenty minutes every day and then gradually walk for thirty minutes five times a week until he could walk comfortably for forty-five minutes to an hour. He would keep track of his time and gradually increase his speed until he could walk four miles easily in an hour.

In addition to those walking goals, the One Minute Manager also decided, if he felt up to it, to mix some jogging in with his walking. He would also try to walk up the stairs at the office rather than taking the elevator when there were five or fewer flights. If he ate out, he would choose a restaurant a couple of blocks from the office so he could walk. His secret was to start "thinking physical." He would walk to the next office to discuss a problem rather than request his people to come to see him or use the phone. An added benefit from this plan was to encourage the One Minute Manager "to manage by wandering around." The One Minute Manager also signed up at his health club for a flexibility and strength training class that met twice a week. Going to the club for these classes would also motivate him to use the other facilities and get in an occasional racquetball or basketball game.

WHILE he was setting up these goals, the One Minute Manager kept thinking about his past New Year's Eve resolution behavior. "I'm great at announcements," he thought, "but lousy at sticking to what I said I was going to do."

When the One Minute Manager shared that concern, the professor suggested he should get someone to agree to be his coach—a person to be his conscience and keep him honest about sticking to his program. While a colleague, friend, or family member could do that, the professor urged him to work with John Turner, the exercise physiologist at the health club he had joined. The professor said, "One of the real benefits of that club is that they have an ongoing coaching process that John heads up. I'll call him and see if he'll work with you himself."

As soon as the One Minute Manager met him, John Turner agreed to work with him. The first thing he did was give the One Minute Manager a copy of *Getting Physical* by Art Turock. He said, "After you read this book you'll realize that my job as your coach is not to tell you what you should do—the professor and your doctor have already done that—but to help you live by your word."

"Live by my word?" echoed the One Minute Manager.

"Yes," said Turner. "From talking to you, I suspect your *fitness motto* should be:

Commitment!

. . . not

announcements,

make the

difference.

"Commitment just means keeping your promises to yourself," continued Turner. "If you say you are going to eat meat only twice a week, or exercise five times a week, then you should do exactly that. How many diets do you think it takes to lose weight?"

"Only the one that you stick to," insisted the One Minute Manager.

"Right. How many exercise programs do you think it takes to get your heart rate and general fitness to a satisfying level?"

"Only the one that you stick to."

"That's my job. To make sure you stick to your guns. I want to meet or talk with you on the phone at least three times a week. Our first meeting should occur at the beginning of the week so we can set weekly eating and exercise goals. I always want to set two different goals: 'No Matter What' and 'Target.' 'No Matter What' goals are ones you commit to accomplish, and 'Target' goals are hoped-for goals you would feel super about accomplishing."

"The second meeting, during the middle of the week, really starts the feedback process, doesn't it?"

"Yes," said Turner. "At that time we can discuss your progress and either praise, reprimand, or redirect your efforts."

"THEN I suppose the last meeting will occur at the end of the week," suggested the One Minute Manager, "and include both an evaluation of the past week and goal setting for the next week. That's a lot of contact, but I think I need close supervision."

"And guess what?" asked Turner.

"What?"

"As soon as you show me you don't need much supervision—when you are keeping your commitment," said Turner, "I will reduce the number of weekly contacts."

"That's a deal."

Then, with the help of his new coach, the One Minute Manager discussed with his family, friends, management team, and staff how they could help him accomplish his goals. If they saw him eating or drinking something he shouldn't, or scheduling a meeting when he should be exercising, what would be helpful?

The One Minute Manager agreed with everyone that it would be helpful if they gave him a praising on the spot if he was making progress. They should tell him what they saw him doing right and how it made them feel. If they caught him doing anything wrong, like ordering an inappropriate dessert or sneaking a high-salt or -sugar snack, they should reprimand him on the spot—tell him what he had done wrong and how they felt about it and then assure him that he was better than that and could stick to his guns. This was important because he knew that:

Feedback
is the
Breakfast of Champions

Praise on the spot . . .

Reprimand on the spot

His family also agreed not to keep the house stocked with tempting goodies and flaunt their ability to eat anything they wanted in front of him. In fact, Alice said that she would help him prepare healthful snacks of fruit and cut-up vegetables. To keep track of his progress, the One Minute Manager decided to keep graphs at both home and office. That permitted him to fill in his graphs ceremonially each week in front of others and, he hoped, to get an "attaboy."

In addition to his three contacts a week with John Turner, the One Minute Manager saw Larry Armstrong at least once a month and the professor more often since he was doing some of his walking at the university facility. Trying to figure out what reward he could give himself at the end of the three-month period if his progress was good, the One Minute Manager and his family decided that he could buy that good set of golf clubs he had wanted for a long time.

Agreeing on all these things ahead of time made the One Minute Manager feel good. He had certainly never done this with any of his past New Year's resolutions. He now had the commitment he felt he needed to win. Everyone knew his goal, the help and support necessary for goal accomplishment were in place, and what was in it for him if he improved was clear to everyone. He was now ready to "go for it."

In his lifestyle program, what that meant was that he would begin to implement his change effort, and he and everyone involved would stick to the agreements they had made.

WITH his preparation work all completed, the One Minute Manager got under way. Even though he had made a "commitment to his commitment," it was not easy. Not only was it tempting to roll over in the morning rather than get up for his morning walk, he felt embarrassed for his neighbors to see him puffing down the street. They would all toot their horns and give him a big smile. He found himself wondering what they were really thinking. While he thought he could survive all this, what really concerned him most were the dogs who roamed free in the neighborhood. Surprisingly, they turned out to be more friendly than he thought they would be.

He would never forget his first exercise class at the health club. When he walked into the weight room he felt everyone was looking at him. It was like having no clothes on. So he sucked in his gut and made one pass through the room.

When he saw that most of the people had gathered for the class, the One Minute Manager sneaked back into the weight room and stood at the back of the class. "I still can't understand what all these thin people are doing here," he thought. As if that wasn't bad enough, when the instructor asked the group to start with some stretching exercises, the One Minute Manager wanted to find a hole to crawl into because he could barely reach his knees. He did not know how he could possibly last for forty-five minutes.

When the class was finally over, the One Minute Manager had survived but his eyes were burning with sweat, the :01 on his T-shirt seemed to be dripping into his belly button, his face was all red, and his muscles twitching. When he finished showering and headed to his car, the One Minute Manager could feel almost every step. It was a real effort just to lift his leg into the car. He undoubtedly had strained not trained. But whatever he had done, when he was finally settled in the car, he felt all alone. All the feelings he had identified in the change exercise at Larry Armstrong's company reappeared to torment him in every part of this first exercise-class session.

As if his exercise program was not tough enough, the One Minute Manager found eating the right things even harder. He began to notice how often commercials on radio and TV, billboards on the road—all suggested eating or drinking something that is bad for you. He found himself thinking about food all the time. The hardest thing was stopping his "grazing behavior," the way he used to go into the kitchen at night looking for something to eat and begin to take a bite out of one thing after another—only to say to himself, "That's not what I really wanted." Now when the One Minute Manager found himself standing in the middle of the kitchen at night, he had to redirect himself to his vegetable and fruit tray. And keeping his agreement to stop drinking—he always seemed to eat more when he drank—was sometimes hard too. He'd never forget the conversation he had about his drinking with his fitness coach, John. After they had talked about his exercise and eating goals for the week, John asked the One Minute Manager about his drinking goals.

"You've been limiting your alcohol consumption when you are around people who are drinking to an occasional glass of wine or substituting orange juice mixed with club soda. How does that sound for this week?"

"This might be a tough week for that," said the One Minute Manager. "My wife and I have former colleagues and old friends visiting for three days this week and they always want to celebrate and party. This might be a bad drinking week."

"WAIT a minute," said Turner. "You seem to be saying that your drinking goal holds only if it's convenient. That doesn't sound like commitment to me. Committed people are unreasonable about accomplishing their goals. If you start finding reasons now not to stick to your goals, then your program will become just that—one of convenience not commitment."

"You got me," said the One Minute Manager. "*So I either have to get bigger than my reasons or I will continue to get bigger*. They'll just have to learn to love me drinking and toasting with my orange juice and club soda mix."

With that kind of accountability and planning every week, the One Minute Manager was able to make some good progress and prevent lapses from turning into an excuse to give up the program completely. That's what had happened to him in the past. He would do fine for a week or so on his eating and then get a "Big Mac attack" and eat everything in sight. One slip would lead to another and another and pretty soon he would rationalize that maybe this was not the right time to be watching his weight.

Or his exercising would be going fine and then a few days of rain would put a dent in it and pretty soon he would be sleeping in again rather than getting up and doing his exercise. By involving others like John Turner, his family, friends, and colleagues in helping him succeed the One Minute Manager was almost immediately confronted by his lapses—and he sure had some. Like the night he innocently headed out around ten P.M. to the local all-night convenience store to get *The Wall Street Journal* and ended up at the diner having a cheeseburger, fries, a piece of blueberry pie à la mode, and three glasses of milk. When he got home, Alice, knowing his past pattern, asked where he had been. Since she was not hostile but caring, he told her what had happened. And then, as everyone in his support group had agreed to do, she said, "Are you going to get back on your program or not?" That question left no room for an "I'll try" answer. And when the One Minute Manager said "Yes," he got instant support and encouragement from Alice. So he learned that a slip in his eating habits was not bad as long as the slip did not turn into an avalanche.

The One Minute Manager loved watching the graphs moving in the right direction and getting the "attaboys" from everyone. At the end of twelve weeks he weighed 207—three pounds less than his intended goal. He was easily able to walk briskly for forty-five minutes. In fact, for three Saturdays he had extended his walk to an hour. While he wasn't able to cover four miles in that time, he felt much better about himself.

AS he reviewed where he had been three months ago on the balance model of autonomy, perspective, connectedness, and tone, the One Minute Manager felt so much better now. Taking the time to exercise daily and work on his tone had not only made him feel better physically and given him more energy but provided him with an increased sense of autonomy or control in his life. To keep doing that, as well as sticking to healthy eating habits, he had to make choices all the time and he found, much to his delight, that he could make the right ones far more often than the wrong ones. Taking that time every day for himself gave him the opportunity to think and get his life back into perspective. The family began to dream together about things they wanted to do and have happen in the future. And finally, he was amazed at how much less affected he was by little hassles and how much more patient and empathetic and connected to the people around him he had become. He had kept his commitment to his commitment and it was rewarding to him.

Even more satisfying was the impact he was having on other important people in his life. Whenever he got a chance, he talked with people about the power of working on their tone and physical well-being as a way of bringing balance to their lives and reducing the potential negative effects of stress. The phone calls from his daughter and a close friend and business associate were worth all the grunting and groaning he had done to begin to get his tone under control.

Just after the One Minute Manager had met the professor and started his program, he visited his oldest daughter, Cathy. At the time she was eight months pregnant and looking forward to her first child. She had recently stopped the junior high school teaching job that she had held for the first two years she and her husband, Alan, had been married. She was fascinated when the One Minute Manager told her about the balance model and the important turnaround role of tone. In fact, she had even taken notes. So her call after almost two months of mothering her delightful baby boy, Jimmy, did not come as a complete surprise.

"Dad, I just had to call and tell you how much the conversation we had several months ago got me out of a deep depression. The weather was even starting to get nice but I wasn't able to pull myself out of this sort of funk I was in until I ran into the notes I had taken from our conversation. Even though I had looked forward to having children, when I looked at my life in terms of your balance model I was in bad shape right now. In terms of autonomy, my life has gone to sub-zero. It seems like I'm nursing Jimmy twenty-four hours a day. Whenever I start a project, I get interrupted. I haven't even sent out the thank-you notes for all the lovely gifts we've gotten. I have lost control.

"In terms of connectedness, I feel tremendously connected to Jimmy. He's the cutest little thing in the world. But as cute as he is, he doesn't carry on much of a conversation. And to add to that, Alan has been busy at work and hasn't been around as much as I thought he would be. And most of my friends don't have kids yet so they're all involved in their work. So I'm basically alone most of the day with no one to talk with or even tell how cute Jimmy is.

"As for perspective, I know this is the best time in my life to have a baby and this kind of intensive child care is not going to last forever—Jimmy is going to grow up and go to preschool and then kindergarten—but we want to have another baby. This could go on for five or six years.

"And then as far as tone goes, forget it! I am fatter than I've ever been in my life. I wish I were still wearing maternity clothes. I have bumps where I never knew you could have bumps.

"What I called to tell you is that I have just joined an aerobics dancing class. When I took a look at my life, I realized from our conversation that the way to turn all this imbalance around is by working on my tone. So I just signed up yesterday. They have a child-care part of their program where I can leave Jimmy during class. And, Dad, I'm feeling better already. By getting myself organized and out of the house three times a week I know I will start to get my autonomy back. In addition, all the new friends I'll meet in the same condition will really help my connectedness. My perspective is already improving. Alan even noticed the difference. In fact, we had a great conversation last night about carving out some time alone together to talk about our lives and the future. So thanks, Dad, you really helped and I wanted you to know it."

The One Minute Manager beamed with pride listening to the excitement in his daughter's voice. And all from deciding to take charge of her life rather than let it happen.

As if the call from his daughter wasn't enough, the call from Hank Barnes, one of his oldest and dearest friends and business associates, was frosting on the cake. Hank was a very successful financial analyst living in New York. Weight had never been a problem for him, so he had been a dedicated nonexerciser for years. When the One Minute Manager had seen him a month before, he really seemed spaced out, though. His success was starting to get to him just as it had been getting to the One Minute Manager. In fact, five times during their lunch together, Hank had excused himself to make a phone call. When the One Minute Manager finally got his attention, he told Hank about his meeting with the professor and his exercise and weight-control program and what it was doing to balance his life. Hank didn't seem that impressed. As least that's what the One Minute Manager had thought until he got the call.

"You probably didn't think I heard what you were saying during our lunch together—about how working on your tone has helped the rest of your life," said Hank. "But I just called to tell you that I did and what I have done about it. You know how I hate exercise, but two weeks ago I decided to try a daily regimen of exercise. I began walking across the Brooklyn Bridge and home each day—that's four miles daily. And what a difference it has made. I've never felt better. In doing that, I found I also liberated myself from the subway! Now I have a five-minute ride on the local each way instead of forty-five minutes (or more!) of pure torture twice a day.

"I suddenly feel that I have control over my time again. Also things aren't bothering me as much. In fact, just yesterday my secretary said everyone is wondering, 'What's happened to Mr. Barnes? He seems to be so calm lately.' And all that quiet time alone has really made me think about my life and what I'm doing with it. And all this because I decided to exercise. Thanks."

The One Minute Manager smiled as he hung up the phone. He realized that he enjoyed playing a role in helping others take control of their lives through attention to health and fitness. As a result, he was even more committed to staying on his own program.

So that he would not revert to old behaviors in terms of his exercise program and would continue to lose weight until his final goal of 175 to 185, the One Minute Manager established new three-month goals with the professor and his doctor. This time, though, he didn't feel that soliciting support from his family, friends, co-workers, and his coach, John Turner, was as important. As he told Turner, "What began as work has become fun. Now exercise seems like an automatic part of my life and eating sensibly has become much easier."

Turner smiled, "What you're essentially saying is that commitment is difficult only when you're doing something you do not want to do."

"THAT'S perfect," said the One Minute Manager. "I've always wanted to be in shape; I just always had good reasons why consistent exercise and diet were impossible. I've proved to myself that the time was always there. What was missing was my commitment to being fit."

"Say more about that," probed Turner.

"Something you said to me in our first meeting stuck with me," said the One Minute Manager. "You mentioned there are no degrees of commitment. Either you are committed, or you're not. Commitment means doing what it takes to get results, no matter what. So when results come slowly, instead of quitting, you redesign your fitness and eating program. When the schedule is ever-changing and a routine workout time is impractical, you use a variety of unusual exercise times but the workouts still get done. When temptations to overeat or indulge occur, you just do what makes sense."

"It sounds as if you're ready to coach yourself," said Turner proudly.

"I'm ready to get started," said the One Minute Manager.

SHORTLY after he began his second three-month period, the One Minute Manager began to evaluate various approaches for a health-promotion program in his company. He found the scope ranged from well-publicized programs like First Chicago, Progressive Insurance Company, Steelcase, UAW/General Motors and Xerox with their million-dollar facilites and full-time professional personnel, to excellent low-cost programs for small and medium-size companies ($2 per employee per month), which include lifestyle-analysis questionnaires, seminars, monthly newsletters, bulletin-board displays, and other health-promotion activities like a company-sponsored fun run.

Since the One Minute Manager was running a medium-size company ($200 million gross sales) he decided to set up a health-promotion program at the lower end of the scale, close to the kind of program Larry Armstrong had. In fact, Larry and the professor helped him get started. They were so proud of the personal progress the One Minute Manager had made with his own program that they knew his company health program would be a real winner, too. And it was.

The personal health and quality-of-life benefits could be clearly observed with his employees within six months. Just as the One Minute Manager had, people began to look and feel better. As a result, people were moving to the right on the lifestyle continuum and feeling more energy and enthusiasm. They seemed to have more balance in their lives and to be able to cope more easily with the stress and strain of the job. And eventually, after a long period of time, the inevitable happened.

THEY PERFORMED BETTER. Not only did the performance improve, but over the years absenteeism and turnover were reduced and the cost of health, life, and worker compensation were significantly lowered. All in all, it was a win-win program. The company's support for health promotion demonstrated top managers' commitment to people, and the people in turn answered with a GREATER commitment to excellence.

Wherever the One Minute Manager went he told people the good news:

In a stress-producing world,
Where it seems
We can't control very much,
We can control
Our own health and lifestyle.

And when we do,
It makes a difference
to both people
and organizations.

Find Out More

In 1979 Ken Blanchard founded The Ken Blanchard Companies to support organisations looking to put the principles of his books into practice. Now a major international management consultancy and training organisation, the company works with many of the world's leading businesses to unleash the full power and potential of their people. The Ken Blanchard Companies is perhaps best known as the originator of the most widely used leadership development process, Situational Leadership® II and also specialises in Team Building, Organisational Change and Customer Service. Consultancy services, in-house training, public workshops, coaching, speakers and a wide variety of learning materials are also provided through a network of offices in 30 countries worldwide. If *The One Minute Manager Balances Work and Life* has inspired you to transform your business, contact:

The Ken Blanchard Companies
Blanchard House
1 Graham Road
Wimbledon
LONDON SW19 3SW

Tel: + 44 (0) 20 8540 5404
Fax: + 44 (0) 20 8540 5464
Email: uk@kenblanchard.com
Website: www.kenblanchard.com

For other worldwide locations visit the Website or contact

The Ken Blanchard Companies
125 State Place
Escondido
California 92029
USA

Tel: (001) 760 489 5005
Fax: (001) 760 489 8407

Praisings

Barby and Ned Doughterty for living an example of a healthy lifestyle.

Glen Hummer for teaching Dee Edington and many others what it takes to become champions.

Spencer Johnson for his continual inspiration as a writer.

Allan Merten for having the vision to add a healthy lifestyle section to the Division of Executive Education at the University of Michigan.

Dick Sarns for caring about the health-related behaviors and quality of life of his employees.

The late **Herb Shepard** for his personal charisma and the initial work on the balance model.

Charlie Smith for teaching us the change exercise.

Eleanor Terndrup for her devotion to this book and the care and efficiency with which she handled all the typing changes that came with each new revision.

Art Turock for teaching us the difference between commitment and interest and the importance of coaching in getting fit.

The folks at BTD for their constant support and feedback. Present and former **students** at the Health Management Research Center for adapting to a rapidly developing field.

The Centers for Disease Control for leading the distribution of the Health Risk Appraisal in the USA.

Larry Hughes at William Morrow and **Margaret McBride**, our literary agent, for their commitment to the One Minute Manager concept.

Everett and Ruth Edington, Ted and Dorothy Blanchard, and **Jim and Natalie McKee** for providing loving, safe, and supportive family environments.

About the Authors

Few individuals have had as much impact on the day-to-day management operations of companies as **Kenneth Blanchard,** coauthor of *The One Minute Manager*® (with Spencer Johnson), *Raving Fans* (with Sheldon Bowles), *Gung-Ho!* (with Sheldon Bowles), and The One Minute Manager® Library.

Blanchard earned his B.A. in government and philosophy from Cornell University, his M.A. in sociology and counseling from Colgate University, and his Ph.D. in administration and management from Cornell University.

As a writer in the fields of leadership, motivation, and management of change, Blanchard's impact has been far-reaching. The text *Management of Organizational Behavior: Utilizing Human Resources,* now in its seventh edition, coauthored with Paul Hersey, is considered standard reading on the subject.

Marjorie Blanchard, co-founder of Blanchard Training and Development, Inc., and coauthor of *Working Well* (with Mark Tager), is a widely known and respected consultant, lecturer, and trainer. She has been a popular faculty resource for the Young Presidents' Organization (YPO) for almost a decade. Chosen as Speaker of the Year in 1983 by *New Woman* magazine and American Express, Dr. Blanchard specializes in the areas of communication, leadership, health promotion, life planning, and team building.

Dr. Blanchard received her B.A. and M.S. degrees from Cornell University and her Ph.D. in communication studies from the University of Massachusetts, Amherst. As director of the Office of the Future, Dr. Blanchard directs the future planning and opportunity development of the company.

D. W. Edington is a professor of kinesiology at the University of Michigan. He is also director of the Management Research Center at the university. He received his B.S. in mathematics and Ph.D. in physical education from Michigan State University, completed postdoctoral work at the University of Toronto, and taught at the University of Massachusetts prior to coming to Michigan in 1976.

Dr. Edington is the author and coauthor of numerous articles and books, including *The Biology of Physical Activity* (with V. Reggie Edgerton) and *Frontiers of Exercise Biology* (with Katarina Borer and Tim White). His work with the Health Risk Appraisal and corporate health evaluation programs is considered to be the model for corporate development plans in the wellness area.

Physical exercise is not merely necessary to the health and development of the body, but to balance and correct intellectual pursuits as well. The mere athlete is brutal and philistine, the mere intellectual unstable and spiritless. The right education must tune the strings of the body and mind to perfect spiritual harmony.—PLATO

HarperCollins Readers' Club

[illegible]

[illegible] Readers' Club today

[illegible]

[illegible]